A CHARMED YOUNG LIFE

Joe

Sadly you are not
in this one, but
enjoy nonth the less

Good to see you

Rick

A CHARMED YOUNG LIFE

NAVIGATING THE CALM 1950's
THROUGH THE TURBULENT 1960's

RICHARD A. MOORE

Printed in the United States of America

First Printing, 2021
Trade Paperback: 978-1-7362313-5-7
EBook 978-1-7362313-4-0

Cover Design and book design: Glen M. Edelstein

This book is dedicated to my father, Lester James Moore, who prepared me for a productive adult life, by example.

CONTENTS

INTRODUCTION

THIS IS THE FIRST book of two. It covers my life through college, 1947-1969. The second book cover my next two years in the army, the first at Fort Belvoir Virginia and the second in Vietnam. When I started writing, my intent was to focus on my time in the army, with a short introduction of my life up to that point. Well, things got out of hand and hence two books. For those people who do not populate these pages, I hope you enjoy the story. For those who do, I hope I got it right, and if not, let me know.

1.

BACKGROUND

CALL ME "ISHMAEL." ACTUALLY, call me Rick. I'll explain in more detail as the story unfolds.

It all began on 7-27-47, a run of 7s which I have never really counted on as good luck, but makes me feel good every time I'm asked to repeat it. Good karma. If life is 50% luck, 40% hard work, and 10% sheer brilliance, then I have made the most of the luck part. Coming of age in the 1950s and 1960s was not a bad place to start. Yes, polio was still around in the '50s, it struck one of my grammar school classmates; and we didn't have 250 TV stations, but growing up in the land of "Leave it to Beaver" and stumbling into the Age of Aquarius was a blessing.

I had the good fortune to miss the Black Plague, the Inquisition, the Depression, and two World Wars. I had the further good fortune of being born in New York City, the center of the universe, riding the post WWII economic boom and the migration to the suburbs. Also of major significance, I was a white male, when that was the equivalent of being born on third base. All this good luck, together with great parents, wise mentors, and good health, is almost embarrassing. I have tried hard not to mess things up.

Suburbia in the 1950s provided neighborhood schools you could walk to and vacant lots you could play on after school, all safe without adult supervision. Doors were not locked, and milk and eggs were delivered by the milkman to your front porch. But big changes were in the making. The car became king, chain motels/hotels sprang up, and McDonalds and rock and roll were born. Computers were being developed, first to fight the Cold War and put men on the moon, and then to be commercialized and change almost everything.

In high school, in the early 1960s, I could hang out at the local pizzeria, buy ONE slice for 25 cents, and listen to "Walk Like a Man" by the Four Seasons. In college, in the second half of the 1960s, I could still listen and dance to great music, get drunk, flunk physics, get drafted, and get a girl pregnant. The last one almost happened but didn't. The others did.

2.

THE FAMILY AND 1950's

BOTH MY PARENTS WERE only children. My father was fine without a big family and would say "you can pick your friends, but you can't pick your relatives."

I never knew my grandfathers, who died long before I was born, and both grandmothers died by the time I was 10 years old. We had a nuclear family, Mom, Dad, my sister Leslie, and me, with little talk of our family tree. The only two stories I remember were on my mother's side of the family. Her father, Harry May, was born in Charleston, SC, which remained a great mystery to us northerners, and remains so today. Her mother's maiden name was Schleiermacher, apparently related to the German reformed theologian and philosopher, Friedrich Danial Ernst Schleiermacher (1768-1834), although an "e" was lost somewhere along the way. There is a statue to Fred in an Austrian village that my sister once visited. Whether the ancestry is true or not, I didn't inherit any of his intellect or passion for religion.

It would have all ended there, except my good friend Mike Hanlon was deeply interested in his ancestry and tracked his family tree to the Mayflower. He convinced me to get on Ancestry.com and track down my grandfather, Harry May, to Charleston. I did, but despite my best efforts couldn't track Harry earlier than his time in Brooklyn, NY.

Mike took up the hunt and he too couldn't trace Harry back to Charleston. He did however dig into my father's side of the family and found that I'm related to John and Priscilla Alden, of Mayflower and Pilgrim fame. This beats Irish potato farmers, but when you find out that there are 35 million descendants from the Mayflower, it's not so impressive, but fun to know.

Now for information I do know and care about.

My father, Lester James Moore, was brought up a Catholic in Brooklyn, New York. When he was born in 1909, Brooklyn had only recently been made a borough of NY City. Before 1898, it was the second largest city in the U.S. with about 3 million people. Brooklyn had a local paper, the Brooklyn Eagle, and of course a local ball team, the Dodgers. More on that later.

My dad went to Brooklyn Tech high school and then right to work for Consolidated Edison (Con Ed), the local power company. College wasn't even considered in those days. In high school, he was president of his fraternity and a good but skinny second baseman who could turn the double play. He hit for average with few home runs and played for many years after high school on the Con Ed team, long before I was born. He also played basketball and had a deadly two-handed set shot that was the style of the day.

Dad hurt his back when I was young, so I rarely saw him play baseball, except once during a father/son ball game when I was about 14. He couldn't run because of his back but made good contact and hit a few singles. I was proud of him. He wasn't brilliant, but by every measure had a well-developed emotional intelligence. People liked and trusted him.

During WWII, Dad was in his mid 30s and as an only child could have avoided the draft. Nevertheless, he enlisted in the Navy and spent the last years of the war in the Pacific on a mine sweeper, the USS Brock. After the Japanese surrendered, the Brock put into port at Nagasaki, a month or so after the atomic bomb. Somehow, on leave, he picked up a Japanese rifle which he took home as a souvenir. It remains one of my treasured possessions.

On shore leave, likely against all rules, he took pictures which show the complete devastation from the bomb and, even today, take your breath away. He wrote captions on the back of each. One picture shows rubble as far as the eye can see, with one concrete building partially standing. In the foreground, a Japanese civilian is standing with his back to the camera relieving himself. His caption was "Jap toilet." I have often wondered if exposure to the radiation might have been a factor in the lung cancer that took him too early at 56. Smoking unfiltered cigarettes might have also contributed (you think?!).

By all accounts, my father's parents' marriage was not a good one. The Depression was hard on my grandfather, who took to drink and became abusive. When my grandmother and father went to the local parish priest for advice and support, they were told: "The man of the house must be obeyed." Simple as that, except it wasn't the answer they were looking for. My father left and never again went into a church, except once when my sister, Leslie, got married. I understand.

His father died in 1940 from the booze, while my parents were on their honeymoon at Niagara Falls. When he got the news by phone, he didn't tell my mother because he knew she would insist on immediately returning for the funeral. Mom apparently had a plan to reconcile her new husband and father-in law. She was very persuasive in this regard, but never had the opportunity. It was sad to end that way, but Dad was a man of strong opinions and his father had burned too many bridges. He was also very much in love with my mother and wanted her to enjoy the trip. I don't know anything else about my grandfather, because my father never talked about him. But more importantly, he did not repeat his father's mistakes.

My father's mother died when I was about 10, but I did get to know her a bit, though from a distance. We moved to New Jersey when I was 3 and Grandma stayed in Brooklyn. She didn't like the suburbs and so didn't visit often. She was a big formidable woman, at least from my point of view, and I never warmed to her -- likely because I was so terribly insecure as a little kid. The one defining remembrance is her coming all the way to NJ, on public transportation, taking me back to Brooklyn to see an afternoon Dodger game and then back to NJ. I think she stayed the night, although she didn't like sleeping in the suburbs; it was too quiet!

As I mentioned, my father was a man of strong opinions; some would say he was to the right of Genghis Khan. Actually, I would have called him a compassionate Republican and if you read about Genghis Khan, you will find him to be a brutal general, but a brilliant, thoughtful, and inclusive administrator of his empire -- the largest in human history. He would have liked my father and vice versa. Dad did not like the Democrats and often associated them with "creeping socialism." If FDR's name came up at the dinner table, you knew you were in for a history lesson delivered with passion. FDR was not the hero in these lessons.

My father's thoughtfulness, on the other hand, is best illustrated by what I'm most proud of, although I didn't know it until after he died. After WWII, the ranks of the American Legion and the Veterans of Foreign Wars were bulging. In our new suburban home in Cresskill, NJ, Dad was approached to join the American Legion several times and always declined. He never said why. You see, at the time, these organizations excluded Blacks and Jews, among others. He was not against organizations that had rules and criteria for acceptance based on merit or talent, but he flatly rejected racial and religious bigotry, especially given his experience with the Catholic Church. This was a progressive approach for the mid 1950s and one with which my mother heartily agreed.

It's not possible to talk about my dad without including sports, especially the Dodgers. In my father's day, baseball was king. Basketball was a distant second and football essentially stopped at the college level. For anyone who lived in Brooklyn, there were two religions: the formal one and the Dodgers. The 1950s were one of the most exciting times in baseball history. For most of the decade there were three teams in NYC and often there were "subway" World Series. The Yankees from the American League and either the Giants or Dodgers from the National League. There were only 8 teams in each league and the NY teams were always in the hunt.

In the early 1950s the Dodgers lost several heartbreaking series, some to the Giants in the National League race, most notably in 1951 when Bobby Thomson hit the home run "heard around the world." But mostly it was the dreaded Yankees who broke your heart. I was too young in the early '50s to understand the game, but I could understand my father's and mother's despair when Dem Bums lost.

By 1955, I was part of the family cheering section and cut school the afternoon the Dodgers won the World Series for the first time in many years. I watched the final few innings at Doug Welty's, because his house was closest to the school. We watched on an early black and white TV with a screen about 8 inches wide and a blurry picture. It was sheer joy to see it and not just listen on the radio.

Dad worked for Con Ed and they had terrific seats in all three stadiums, so we went to a lot of games. The best seats were at Yankee Stadium, right behind the dugout on the third base line. I didn't realize how good we had it. But my most memorable game was a night game at Ebbets Field. The Con Ed seats were in the mezzanine over first base and given how small the field was, you were literally hanging over the first base coach. Great seats. The game in question was between the Dodgers and the St Louis Cardinals. It was a high scoring game, since by the 9th inning Stan "The Man" Musial (Cardinals) had hit three home runs and Roy "Campy" Campanella (Dodgers) had hit 2. The Dodgers were behind by 3 runs as they came up in the bottom of the 9th and people began leaving the stadium.

The Dodgers started clawing back, scored one run, and people began coming back to their seats. The crowd was going wild with everyone on their feet screaming. Dad, who wasn't about to leave early, was one of the first on his feet. I was amazed at his enthusiasm and soon all four of us (Dad, Mom, Leslie, and me) were on our feet screaming. Campy came up again, two runs behind, two outs, and two men on base. Not to be outdone by Stan the Man, he hit his third homer and won the game. Today they call it a walk off home run. We were too hoarse to talk on the ride home, but this was the best of the best.

Those Brooklyn Dodgers, Campy (2), Duke Snyder (8), Pee Wee Reese (6), Jackie Roberson (5), Carl Ferrilo (9), Gil Hodges (3), Junior Gilliam (4), and Don Newcome (1) were "The Boys of Summer" so well described by Roger Kahn years later.

In the later '50s and early '60s, there weren't many ball games on TV. One baseball game each on Saturday and Sunday afternoons. Dad loved to watch, but I didn't because of my short attention span. What kept me interested was Dad's knowledge of the game and the things I learned while listening to him describe what was happening. He would start strong, but usually after a beer or two would doze off by the 3rd inning. Then I would go out and play.

When the word leaked that the Dodgers were moving to LA, the reaction was just short of the one after JFK's assassination. It tore the heart out of Brooklyn. The agony was felt most deeply by Dad, but we all grieved. I understood for the first time how much Mom cared about the team.

Speaking of my mother, you couldn't have gotten a better one. Althea Josephine May was a smart kid, skipped a grade, and graduated high school a year early. Her father died when she was 7 in an accident at work. He was a mechanic and a truck he was working on slipped off its support blocks and crushed him.

As noted, my grandfather, Harry May, was born in Charleston, SC and moved north presumably for work. My grandmother, Nana to Leslie and me, worked in a florist shop and my mom started working there to make ends meet after her father died. Mother was encouraged to go to college by her teachers, but it was out of the question financially.

After high school, Mom got a job at Con Edison where she met Lester. She was 7 years younger, which was common at that time. Today she would have gone on to college and been successful at whatever she did. You see, in addition to being smart, she had an even more well-developed emotional intelligence than Dad. She was a liberal Democrat who could have debated my father to a standstill, but wisely chose not to. She was much better at getting her point across in more subtle ways. She could see both sides and was an accomplished negotiator on domestic and other issues. Today she would have been comfortable and effective in the most delicate State Department negotiations.

When Leslie was in college, she would bring friends home for a visit. After a bit, the girls began calling Mom "Big Al" despite her small stature, as a term of endearment. It became clear that many of them felt more at home at our house than at their own. Mom was a good listener and was not judgmental. She respected everyone on their own terms, regardless of race, religion, nationality, politics, or sexual preference. She was curious, open-minded, and way, way ahead of the times, especially with regard to lifestyle issues. I took it for granted at the time, but it was quite remarkable. Leslie and I have benefited from her example.

Mother was involved in church and town affairs, including the Cresskill Board of Education. More on that later, but early on she got involved as a volunteer supporting the schools. As part of this, she arranged for a woman speaker to make a presentation to the PTA. I didn't understand this until much later, but the woman was on the far left of the political spectrum, a socialist, and spoke as one. This horrified the more conservation section of the peanut gallery, and Mom got what amounted to hate mail. She had the courage of her convictions and the turmoil passed.

In summary, Leslie and I couldn't have had better parents. They imparted their values by living them, doing the right thing when no one was watching, and prepared us to be responsible adults, even if we didn't always measure up. They were, and always will be, our quiet heroes.

My sister, Leslie, was born in 1942 before my dad went in the Navy, and I was born in 1947 after he came back. My arrival didn't sit well with Leslie, as it meant competition. The fact that I was a cute little redheaded kid didn't help either. We fought pretty much from the time I could throw a punch until she left for college. Although there was much internal strife, which sorely tested my parents' patience, the wagons were circled when there was a threat from outside. My sister was ready to protect me from schoolyard bullies at any cost.

Once she left for college, we buried the hatchet and became fast friends. Both of us were born in Brooklyn and moved to NJ in 1950 when I was 3. My only memory of Brooklyn was of Leslie catching fireflies in our postage stamp backyard on a hot summer night and smearing them to expose the glow. An exploitation of what little nature there was in Brooklyn at the time.

I recently visited the street where I was born in Flatbush, at the end of the D train. It hasn't changed much in 70 years.

3.

CRESSKILL, NEW JERSEY

I WENT THROUGH SCHOOL (K-12) all while living in Cresskill, NJ. The 1950s was the first decade since the roaring '20s that people felt a real sense of optimism. Jobs were back, wages were increasing ahead of inflation, and the great migration to the suburbs began with the promise of your own house and backyard to enjoy the fruits of the American Century, a term coined by Henry Luce in Time magazine.

My parents followed the promise from Brooklyn to 103 Union Avenue, Cresskill, New Jersey. We moved in 1950 when the house cost $10,000. I don't know what the down payment was, but the remainder was financed with a 20-year mortgage. I do remember my mother's great joy in 1971, when the mortgage was paid off.

New Jersey and Long Island received most of the out migration from the city, with Connecticut in third place. My father never spoke of the move, but I often wonder how he felt about leaving the city. Like his mother, I suspect he was a bit bothered by the quiet, at least at first. That is to say nothing of the commute. He took a bus from the top of Union Avenue, 3 houses away, to the Port Authority on the west side of Manhattan, and then a second bus cross town to his Con Ed office one block south of the United Nations on the East River. And this was before the buses had AC. But he never complained.

On summer evenings, just before 5:30 pm, I would go to the corner and wait for the bus and we would walk home together. On really hot days the windows in the bus were open for some air and he would get off with his coat off and tie loose, which was more often than not, a bow tie. These short walks were the highlight of my long summer days. I would bring a rubber ball and we would play a crazy game of catch on the way down Union Avenue.

Once home it was dinner at the kitchen table, all four of us. Mom was a good cook, although that all escaped me at the time. Food prices were reasonable and there was always meat (not much fish), a potato or equivalent, and a vegetable. It was the last part I had trouble with, but the rules were clear about cleaning your plate. Leslie was OK with veggies and it was my constant hope that I could figure a way to transfer my veggies to her plate. One of the few cases where she would have put up with my antics. Sadly, I never figured out a plan that had a chance of working.

When it was just the four of us at dinner, which was most of the time, conversation was about the day's activities and the weather, rather bland. My parents didn't fight and if there was conflict, it was typically because of something Leslie or I did that needed to be exposed.

On Sunday, Mom, Leslie, and I would go to church. Dad read the paper while we were gone and at 1 pm we all had Sunday dinner in the dining room, often with guests. The menu was usually pot roast, mashed potatoes, and a vegetable or some other comfort food. My father, a good Englishman, liked his food well-cooked. I didn't realize you could have a medium rare steak until I was well into high school.

I didn't like Sunday dinner much, since I couldn't go out to play until dinner was over. One advantage was Sunday supper, the evening meal. Because we had our main meal mid-day Sunday, we often had pancakes or French toast (breakfast food) for Sunday supper. My Mom's pancakes were not out of an Aunt Jemima box. She mixed flour, milk, and eggs in a magic formula that resulted in a thin paste. Once cooked on a very hot skillet, you essentially had a crepe. Wonderful.

Leslie and I always looked down on the standard "fat" pancakes and I have never eaten them.

In the summer, Dad would roll out the grill and many a meal was cooked over charcoal. Dad was a stickler for safety, something that came, I think, from Con Ed. If someone screwed up working on electric lines, people could get killed, and they did. Strangely, the concern for safety didn't extend to the grill. To light the charcoal, he would take the gas can for the lawn mower and pour gas on the charcoal, stand back a foot or two, and throw in a lighted match. A small explosion followed, but the fire got started. There might have been a few eyebrows lost along the way.

We lived in a small house which had three bedrooms and one bath when we moved in. The master bedroom was in the front of the house off the living room, and the other two bedrooms and bath were off a hallway from the kitchen in the back of the house. For the first several years, while my grandmother lived with us in one of the rear bedrooms, Leslie and I shared the other room. This was not an appropriate way to encourage good behavior. There was constant bickering, mostly about the imaginary line down the middle of the floor, which we were not allowed to cross by mutual agreement. How our parents got through this period, I do not know.

Sadly Nana passed away, but this allowed us to have separate rooms. Shortly after that, the attic was fixed up as a bedroom for Leslie until she went away to college and then it passed to me. Now, the attic had a pitched roof. There was enough room, just barely, for me to stand in the middle at the peak. As you moved to either side the head room quickly diminished. The workmen put sheet rock on the ceiling down to a point about four feet above the floor and then squared off the room. The new room extended from the back wall about three quarters the length of the house, with the remaining portion left as an unfinished attic for storage. The bed and desk were shoved against the short walls, with just enough head room to sit. It was a big room diminished by the sloping ceiling and the stairway entrance right in the middle. However, for a teenager it had the most important ingredient...privacy!

One more thing about this room. There were two small windows side by side looking out to the backyard. They were double hung windows but had no sash to hold the windows in place. When you opened them, they either got stuck to stay open or you needed to place a book or ruler to hold the window up. Once I opened the window to get a ball that was stuck in the gutter from some backyard ball game. I jammed the window open hoping it would stay, but during my retrieval activities it broke loose and came down not unlike a guillotine. Unfortunately, I had one hand on the windowsill, but fortunately I also had a broom handle on the sill, which was slightly larger in diameter than my fingers. Were it not for the broom handle taking the blow, I likely would have fewer than 10 fingers today.

So, after some weeks of construction, the attic was transformed to Leslie's new bedroom and I was notified that it was strictly off limits for me. To compensate, the bedroom she vacated on the first floor became the TV room and we were in middle-class heaven.

Speaking of TVs, I remember we were one of the last on the block to get one in the early '50s. It was put in the living room, since Nana was still alive. The early TVs were big boxes with a tiny screen and lots of vacuum tubes in the back. Programming didn't start until about 4:30 in the afternoon, when we waited impatiently for the black circle to flip 10, 9, 8, etc. We were actually lucky to be in metro NYC, with the three major networks and a few local ones. I remember one vacation visiting my parents' friends in Williamstown, MA, and finding out to my horror that they had only two stations. How things have changed.

Now to the bathroom, the one bathroom! Actually, I didn't have nearly as much problem with this as Leslie, since my standard of cleanliness was a bit primitive in those days. Other than having to wait to pee, or worse, when someone else was using the john, there were two major problems. The first, which actually had nothing to do with having one bathroom, was the small capacity of the water heater. Until this was upgraded late in the game, you couldn't reliability take two showers in a row, unless you wanted to end the second one with cold water. The horrible forewarning as the water cooled and you frantically tried to rinse off, remains with me to this day.

The second and more frustrating, was the shower itself, or what passed as a shower. We had a cast iron tub, a collector's item today, on one side of a tiny bathroom. There was an oval hoop slightly smaller than the tub about 6 feet high, directly overhead, supported by a vertical post at the faucet end of the tub. A hose, starting at the faucet, snaked up the vertical support to a shower head at the top. At the lower end of the hose was a rubber fitting that was jammed onto the faucet, thus allowing water to pass out the faucet, through the rubber fitting, up the hose to the shower head.

We had poor water pressure, which was another annoyance, especially for the ladies, but it was still enough to highlight the weak link in this whole Rube Goldberg contraption: the rubber fitting connected to the faucet. With the slightest adjustment of the hot or cold water, or no adjustment at all, this connection separated and the water from on high stopped. This routinely happened while washing your hair with suds everywhere. Alas, this fundamental weakness was never properly corrected. Fortunately, when I got to high school and started playing sports, I took my daily shower in the locker room.

The rest of the house had an eat-in kitchen, with century-old appliances and a pantry. The dining and living rooms were standard rectangles. There was a full covered front porch which was well used on hot summer nights, when sleeping inside was difficult. There was also a one car detached garage in the back and a deep grassed backyard. The best part of the backyard was its direct connection to a patch of woods that remained undeveloped until I was in college. When I was little, I was afraid of everything, but especially the monsters in the woods. As I got older, the woods were a great play area and a shortcut to grammar school and Ackerman Dairy.

Between the backyard and Ackerman Dairy was an open area where you could play ball, but the best part was the Dairy itself. Actually, it was just a building that included a huge, refrigerated room where the milk and dairy products were dropped off in bulk and then distributed by the milkmen. Yes, this was the time when milk and eggs were delivered to your front porch every few days by your friendly milkman.

The front door of the dairy building was never locked so customers could just walk in, open the freezer door, and take what they needed if they ran out of their standard delivery. You recorded what you took on a sign-in sheet. It worked on the honor system and you were billed accordingly. I made many trips to the freezer for Mom, and occasionally for me, after an afternoon of playing ball. You see, there was chocolate milk in the refrigerator, the best in the world.

Now back to the house, and the last room: the basement, which was totally unfinished and home to many spiders. My father had a work bench, but he didn't do much handyman stuff, unless something was broken and needed immediate attention. He had the usual complement of tools, and a few cool ones that he somehow got at Con Ed. He never explained. My favorite was a big vice, bolted to the work bench, that could hold anything. I loved to work/play with the tools and once didn't clean up properly after some work. Dad read me the riot act about taking care of your tools. Good advice I remember still.

These were the days before planned obsoleteness, when you fixed things that broke. You didn't just go out and buy a new one. I spent quite some time at the work bench cutting, banging, drilling, and screwing...by myself. I would have been a good carpenter or plumber (not electrical), if I had taken another path later in life.

Another thing I did well was shoveling coal into the furnace. During most of the 1950s, we had a huge coal fired furnace in the basement. The coal truck would come every so often, back into the driveway, put a chute through the cellar window, raise the bed of the truck, and dump the load in the coal bin. It was then Leslie's job, and mine, to keep the fire going during the cold winter months. With white paint, Leslie added a note to the side of the coal bin: "A shovel a day." The arrival of the coal truck was a big event in my young, simple life.

The cellar wasn't a pretty place to work. In the early days, we didn't have a clothes dryer, just a clothes washer in one corner of the basement. So, Mom washed the clothes, carried them out the basement door to the backyard, and hung them on a line to dry. This worked on all but the coldest days, when the clothes froze. So, she hung them in the basement. I always wanted to use the tools to finish the basement and make the workspace more pleasant, but never got around to it.

One day the washer broke down. My father's approach, as a good Republican, was to begin to save enough money so a new washer could be bought with cash. He was not a big fan of debt. My mother could adjust to almost anything, so she began to bring the clothes to the laundromat down the street -- until one day the laundromat dryers also didn't work. She bought the wet clothes back home, said some words we had never heard her say before, and we got a new washer AND dryer that next day. My father had strong convictions but was not stupid.

That was the day of Mom's great explosion. Dad's happened one weekend when he was painting the kitchen. He was a few rungs up the latter painting a wall with a roller when he ran out of paint. The first two steps down were fine, but the last step landed in the paint can and upended it. Not a pretty sight. As the word spread, everyone headed for the hills as he cleaned things up swearing under his breath all the time. It was a contained explosion, but nonetheless intense. Can't tell you how many times we all laughed about that later on, but certainly not during the event.

Christmas was our biggest holiday by far. We had a small cardboard manger scene which had 25 dropdowns that you opened one day at a time starting December 1st. In grammar school 25 days seemed like an eternity, but at least the countdown started. Getting the tree was a big deal, which was done about two weeks before Christmas, but it stayed in the garage until the day before Christmas Eve.

Decoration of the tree was a well-prescribed ritual. We set it up in the same corner on the living room every year and put on the same set of ornaments, with an angel on top that had been handed down from Nana. This all normally went rather well, until it was time to put on the tinsel, the last step. Our approach, which was strongly enforced by Leslie, was to use the thin strands, many of them, and to put them on one by one so they hung freely. This was a slow process that did not favor my impatience. I often tried to put a bunch on at once, to Leslie's great displeasure. These were summarily removed to be replaced one by one. Often there were "words" and often I just gave up and did something else, like eat Christmas cookies. The tree was taken down New Year's Day -- all that work for a week with the tree!

We were allowed to open one present on Christmas Eve, and for me it was always the one from Aunt Dot and Uncle Ed. They always got me clothes that I didn't like, so this was a disappointing start. Mom and Dad put our presents out after we went to bed and it was a big surprise on Christmas morning. We were kept in bed by looking through our stockings and then came the big entrance to the living room. We were always pleasantly surprised.

There was, however, one Christmas when we were told that it had been a difficult year financially and not to have high expectation on Christmas morning. I don't remember being disappointed, but expectations were low. Keep in mind that during the late '50s Dad had a good white-collar job at Con Ed., but only made about $10,000/year. Given the reasonable cost of living at the time, we never wanted for anything of importance. Clearly, Mom and Dad watched expenses, but we rarely felt the pressures.

We lived on the main street in Cresskill, Union Avenue. Our end of the street was residential, and the other end was the commercial downtown. The usual small town stores, including a barber shop, candy store with soda fountain, bakery, drug store, laundry, florist, hardware store, and post office. This cluster of small stores slowly expanded up the street toward us, first with a supermarket and then with a new town hall and library. My parents thought this was a good idea, mostly because of the convenience. For years, every Sunday morning before the rest of us would wake up, my father would walk to the bakery and bring home fresh pastries made on site, the likes of which I haven't tasted since. Many years later after Dad died and Leslie and I were long gone, Mother sold the house to make room for a small office building.

4.

MERRITT MEMORIAL SCHOOL, K-6TH GRADE

ALL THROUGH THE 1950S, I could walk to school in five minutes or stroll down the street and get an ice cream sundae with whipped cream and a cherry at Dave's for 25 cents -- the best treat imaginable. And if you had a few pennies left in the bottom of your pocket, there was a vast array of penny candy.

It was like living in a sitcom, somewhere between Father Knows Best and the Andy Griffin Show. Our parents had a great marriage and were open-minded people, but below the surface in the community there was corrosive bigotry related to race, sexual orientation, and religion. There were no black kids in my class and only a few in the whole school system. The black families all lived on an unpaved street, one of the few in town. I never connected the dots as to why this was so. Every gay kid was in the closet, and we made fun of gay folks in general. This was essentially taught by our churches, along with a whole bunch of other hypocritical stuff. You were apparently only to love certain neighbors, the ones that looked and thought like you. Mercifully, I was oblivious to most of this until much later.

Grammar school was difficult for me given that I was afraid of my own shadow and mildly dyslexic. Let's face it, I was a momma's boy with little or no confidence, something that slowly changed over time with experience and interaction with my schoolmates. Being mildly dyslexic didn't help (a huge understatement). Keep in mind that my condition didn't have a name in the 1950s, at least not a medical term. It did have a name or names, depending upon how delicate you wanted to be. On the soft side, you were a slow learner or more brutally, "retarded."

Before kindergarten, I was protected at home and in the backyard, except for the monsters. Outside of home I stuck close to my mother. I was definitely not inquisitive or a risk taker and not interested in what was behind a closed door. It could scare me! The main crises at home occurred when my parents had guests over. Mostly I just hid in my room and maybe showed my face quickly before bedtime. One time, Pastor Seiferd and his wife came over and I refused to come out and meet them, cowering behind my dresser. It was a great disappointment to my parents.

Then came the big change: forced social interaction in kindergarten. I made it to school the first day without a complete breakdown, thanks to my mother's considerable talents in positive persuasion. Once there, I was clueless, having no idea what to do or how to do it. It was a big treat to do finger painting and everyone wanted to get their chance, since only a few could do it at one time. I avoided it at all costs, because I knew it was important to clean up and I didn't know how to do it. My goal was to be invisible so as not to bring attention my way. To make matters worse, I began to realize that my reading and writing skills were far weaker than the rest of the pack. This made being invisible all the more important and difficult.

I went to Merritt Memorial School K-6th grade. The only positive thing I can remember inside the school walls was my role as chief projector operator during the 5th and 6th grades. Anytime a teacher wanted to use the projector, I set it up and operated the film. I knew all the tricks to keep it running as the big reel of film chattered through the many spools and guides onto the empty retrieving reel. I was proud of my skills. It was pretty easy and I loved getting out of my regular class to do my magic.

But my overall experience in the classroom from kindergarten to 8th grade followed a general pattern: major inadequacies in spelling, writing, and reading skills, the heart of a grammar school education. Strangely, because I had such low expectations when I was young, later successes seemed so much more wonderful. The opposite of a young brilliant kid who doesn't meet expectations later in life, with the accompanying disappointment.

A girl moved to Cresskill and entered our 6th grade class. As I remember, she was cute as a button with reddish-blond hair and maybe freckles. This description is rendered given the fact that I can't remember her name. In any event, from the very beginning I was an admirer from afar. My finest moment came in the Spring, when I hit a home run playing one of our Little League games at the field behind Merritt Memorial. I know she was there at the beginning of the game, but no one I knew sighted her in the bleachers at the moment of my blast.

The thought of actually asking her if she saw me trotting around the bases was beyond comprehension, in part because I wanted to believe she was there. This just made my puppy love more intense, until I learned she was moving away at the end of the school year. I don't remember if I said goodbye the last day of school, or if she would have cared, but I do remember the next day. It was raining and at one point in the morning I stood at the front door looking out and wondering, if by good fortune, her car would pass for one more glance. I could not stop thinking that the clouds in my life would not part and the rain would never stop. The next day was sunny and fixed my gloom.

All through grammar school I didn't want to go to Merritt Memorial when I got up in the morning. I often tried to convince my mother that I was sick, but it rarely worked. After all it was only a 5-minute walk out the backyard, through two fields, and into class. With my poor academic performance, I had many dark days. The bright spots, and they were considerable, were home life, where I didn't get much shit about my poor grades. My parents thought I was a slow kid, accepted it, and did their best to make me feel worthy. I also had some good friends, which I'll tell you about.

5.

FRIENDS

HOWARD "TRIP" LAW, HARVEY Rosenfeld, and Mike Janiak were my best K-6 friends. Especially Trip, who I met in kindergarten and is still a good friend. How Trip got his nickname remains a mystery. His full name is Howard Goodrich Law III, so you might think the III became triple, shortened to Trip. Not so according to his parents and sister, who should have known, but never gave me a straight answer. He tripped often, not because he was particularly clumsy, which he was, but because his mind was so often somewhere else. Regardless, almost any name was better than Howard in grammar school. Unfortunately, he now uses Howard, which has long been difficult for me to accept.

Trip was smarter than I was, which wasn't hard, but he was socially inept. I was pretty socially inept too, the difference being he didn't care. He was a young absent-minded professor. This was a problem for his mother, Sally, who was Junior League through and through. Sally liked me because I was more compliant, so I spent a lot of time at their house. Two cute little blond boys who played well together with their constant companion: the Law's black lab, Danny. The best dog in the world.

It was hard to compare any dog to Danny. We had two dogs by the time I was 10. The first one was a beagle, Tinker. I loved him, but unlike Danny, he would run away if not on a leash. Tinker was great inside, but less so outside. He got sick when he was only about 6 years old and had to be put down. I tried to be a tough guy when Mom told me the sad news, but quickly went to my room and cried. It was my first close experience with loss. I got over it quickly and we soon got another dog.

The second dog, Sandy, was the cutest pup in a litter from a neighbor's dog. Sandy was that color and we thought we had the pick of the litter. Things soon turned sour. Sandy was wound tighter than a drum and never slowed down. He gave new meaning to the term hyperactive and for his size, he could jump. He was a little guy, less than 10 pounds, but could jump from the floor to the kitchen table.

One day Sandy was home alone with a gate about 4 feet high between him and the kitchen, surely high enough to keep him out. Somehow he got over, went up onto the kitchen table and ate a pound of chop meat on the table thawing for dinner. He had a bit of a tummy ache. The vet pronounced Sandy crazy and that was the end of Sandy. He had created so much tension in the family that we all were quietly happy with the decision. So much for pets. Now back to Trip.

The Laws moved from a small house to a larger one on Lambs Lane, the best address in town at the time. It was a nice house, not huge, on a pretty lot. Most of the other houses on Lambs Lane, a dead end narrow road, were much bigger. The biggest was Dr. Halstead's near the end of the Lane. It was a huge English Tudor as I remember, and Dr. Halstead had a son who Trip knew. Occasionally, when the son was not off at boarding school or traveling the world with his parents, we would go up and play. Not because we particularly liked the son, whose name I forget, but because of Pirate, their Newfoundland. Pirate, about twice the size of Danny, had a friendly disposition and the two dogs loved to play together.

Pirate didn't get too many opportunities to run around, except with us. The house had a huge lawn where we would run around with the dogs and play football. This was great fun except when Pirate got overly excited. He would tackle you and start to make love. Keep in mind Pirate had to be at least 150 pounds and once he got on top of you it was panic time. You only played with Pirate in a group, so there was help to extract you from his grip. We loved Pirate and laughed a lot, despite, or maybe because of, his inappropriate behavior.

There were two other homes on Lambs Lane of note to me, although I don't believe I ever met the owners. One had a pool where we could swim on occasion when the owners were away. The pool fit into the landscape and the bottom was some form of asphalt, at least it looked and felt like asphalt. Several times I got bad scrapes on my knuckles, elbows, and knees as we played around.

I was better at sports than Trip, except for swimming. He could swim faster and hold his breath longer. I hated it when he beat me either underwater or on the surface. But swimming in the Lambs Lane pool was idyllic.

The second house had a paddle tennis court that could be used through the winter. It was clearly an upper-class game and the house was owned by a stockbroker. I didn't understand what it meant at the time, but he had a seat on the NY Stock Exchange. The way Mr. Law explained it in hushed tones suggested to me that this was a big deal. I could beat Trip at paddle tennis and the fact that you could play in cold weather seemed very cool to me, literally. Trip didn't like it as much as I did, so we didn't play often, but when we did, I envisioned myself a titan of Wall Street.

The folks on Lambs Lane were big on sending kids off to boarding school and summer camp, ideally for the whole summer. I suspect social standing and money had something to do with this. After all, at cocktail parties you needed to make sure everyone knew your little darlings were getting the best there was to offer. God forbid they should go to public schools. My parents were huge supporters of public schools but thought it might be worthwhile to send me to summer camp. This idea might have started with Sally, who likely needed a break from Trip during the long hot summers in North Jersey. Trip also loved the idea of getting away from "Sally World."

It was decided that Trip and I would go to camp for two weeks. We were 8 years old. Two weeks sounded to me like a life sentence, at what was either a Boy Scout or YMCA camp, I can't remember. It makes no difference, I hated every second. It gave new meaning to the term homesick. I was afraid to swim, make crafts, sing camp songs, or take a shit, you name it. Even sports, which I was good at, terrified me for some reason. And swimming was the worst. I was afraid of the water and could barely swim. Trip was a fish. At the start of camp, you had to swim a short distance to determine what group you were in. Same results as school, which didn't build my confidence.

The second year, I got to the camp bus to leave for my two weeks in the gulag and refused to get on. My mother's positive persuasion didn't work this time, so we went home. My parents were terribly disappointed and I suspect wondered how I was to grow up and be a functioning adult.

One Halloween, Trip and I decide we would do a costume together. The idea was to be Dr. Frankenstein and his monster. Given our personalities, you would think that Trip should have been the scientist, but alas it was the other way around. I guess I wanted to be the brains for once, since I never was in school, but things didn't turn out well for me. We spent all our efforts on the monster costume, made out of a big box with lots of dials and switches for the body and a smaller box for the head. There was a cord attaching the monster, Trip, to the scientist, me, with a "control" box to keep the monster out of mischief. The problem was we didn't spend any time on my costume, which was weak, not much more than street clothes. As we paraded around outside on the Merritt Memorial basketball court for the judges, most people didn't make the connection between the monster and the scientist. Despite the cord, people liked Trip's costume and didn't quite know what to make of me. I was pissed, having done half the work and getting none of the credit. In a subtle way, it demonstrated, incorrectly, that brawn is more important than brains, at least in a popularity contest.

This highlights the second thing that was so important about my relationship with my friends and the other kids on the playground. I was well-coordinated and a pretty good athlete on the ball field, but, in the classroom, I was the last to be picked for the spelling bee team and the first to sit down. It was often the reverse on the ball field.

Athletics were a casual thing with friends early on, but gave me some victories to counter the classroom defeats. In short, it prevented my self-confidence from going to zero. You don't know how lonely it is to be the last to be picked for a spelling bee team and the first one to miss an easy word. You leave your team and sit down at your desk while everyone else on both teams are standing against opposite walls still playing.

Being a good schoolyard athlete became more important once I got old enough to play Little League. I was born in July a little earlier than most of the other boys in my grade. Since the cut off for Little League was August 1st, I was eligible to play a year earlier than most of the other boys -- by 4 days. So, I went to the tryouts, with all the other kids from 8 to 12 years of age who weren't already on a "major" league team. You were either picked for one of these teams or you played in the "minor" leagues.

Ackerman Dairy, the one behind our house, sponsored a team. I think there were 8 teams. The coach for Ackerman Dairy gave me a choice. I was good enough to make the team, but because I was young, I wouldn't play much. He suggested it might be better for me to join a minor league team and get more opportunities to play.

I knew by the way my father and the coach were talking that the minor league option was the right choice, so I said OK. My father took me for an ice cream cone as a reward for making the right decision, even though I didn't want to. A day or two later, I was watching a game and the Ackerman Dairy coach came up to me and said he had an unexpected opening on the roster and would I consider coming on board. I said yes in a NY minute and was on cloud 9. At 8 years old, by 4 days, I was in the Big Leagues! Suddenly I didn't care if I could spell or read. My father made no protest, and the deed was done.

Because I was the youngest player, I became friends with kids a year older. Two of the best were Dwight Linnemeyer and Sal Rizzo. Dwight was the best pitcher in the league and Sal was his catcher. I played three years with them in Little League and then went on to play several more in Babe Ruth league. During Little League, my favorite place was Dave's candy store just down Union Avenue in the retail section of town.

I was enough of a regular that occasionally Dave would let me stock the candy. The 5 and 10 cent variety above and the penny candy below, behind well-used sliding glass doors. I can picture the display like it was yesterday, because it was perhaps the first job I had. Paid not in coin, but in merchandise of a value not to exceed 5 cents. Dave had a keen sense for business.

One day, one summer, Dwight, Sal, and I came into the store after Dwight had thrown a no-hitter for Ackerman Dairy. Sal gave Dave an inning by inning account of the game and Dave gave each of us an ice cream cone in honor of Dwight's achievement and based on Sal's riveting account. For that moment, Dave took off his business hat and was just a thoughtful grownup. This, for 11-12-year-old Little League kids, was better than a ticker tape parade down Union Avenue.

In Cresskill, back in the '50s, football and basketball weren't as well-organized as baseball. Organized sports were all about baseball, so getting into Little League was a big deal. You played football and basketball in pick-up games with your friends outside. You certainly didn't have football equipment, so playing tackle was a tough afternoon. Basketball was easier, but it was all outside, typically in 3 on 3 games on half court. We had no gym at Merritt Memorial.

Harvey wasn't much of a ball player, but we got along well and played often through grammar school. His father was our dentist and had his office attached to their house. It was a much nicer house than ours, so we spent a lot of time in their TV room. Harvey had an older brother, David, who was my sister's age. Since they were 5 years older, we didn't see much of them. The Rosenfelds observed all the Jewish holidays and sometimes I was part of festivities. Mrs. Rosenfeld was a wonderful Jewish mother and it helped me to appreciate their rituals.

We all went to Dr. Rosenfeld for our teeth and I went often since my attention to brushing was weak, something I regret to this day. It's surprising I wasn't better at oral hygiene for two reasons. First, Leslie shamed me about my "yellow" teeth and I should have listened to her.

Second and more dramatically, in the mid '50s good old Doc Rosenfeld didn't use Novocain. He had a fast drill and a slow drill. The fast one came first and was horrible, but the final touches with the slow drill were out of a medieval horror chamber. I wager if his dentist chair was still around, my handprints would be embedded on the arms of the chair. I can still hear the sound of the slow drill and it gives me shivers. Fortunately, novocaine came on the scene quickly and the torture was over, but my teeth continued to deteriorate.

Trip went away to private school and Harvey and I grew apart after middle school. Mike became my closest friend until mid-high school when he dropped out. Mike at 15 was about 6'2" and 220 pounds, a big boy. The funny part, although not so funny as you will see, is that he was almost that size at 10. He was a good friend to have because no one fucked with us due to his size. The problem was, he had a terrible temper. I never knew his father, who left when he was little and moved to Connecticut. Early on Mike would visit him, but that ended before high school. Maybe a father around would have helped him control his temper, but I doubt it.

Mike had street smarts but wasn't good in school. I think he just didn't care and had no one to tell him otherwise. He was good at sports mostly due to his size, but if things didn't go right, he would explode. If it was a pickup game, all the guys dove for cover. If it was an organized game, like Little League with parents present, things got messy because even the men gave him a wide berth. If he struck out and got pissed, he would smash the bat or throw a ball anywhere. Soon he was unofficially banned from playing. When I started high school, my father didn't think Mike was a good influence and wanted me to stay away from him. I resisted, but when he dropped out of school it became easier. I also was consumed with school, sports, other friends, and soon girls.

My father, God bless him, tried to help Mike and suggested, among other things, that he take the "10 second time out" to calm down when his temper got the best of him. In Mike's case, it would have taken more like 60 seconds. One of my favorite temper stories occurred one winter night when he was coming over to visit. He cut through the back woods and as he came around the corner of our garage, he slipped on ice and landed on his hip...hard. He arrived at the back door looking like a mad man needing to kill something or someone. As he explained his mishap through clenched teeth, I headed to the basement to get a 5-foot-long straight metal bar about an inch in diameter. It looked like a dark heavy spear and I told him to "kill" the ice, not me. Mike took it to the offending ice patch and proceeded to smash the ice to pieces. In the process of letting out his rage he bent the bar at about 45 degrees and broke into a sweat, despite the 25-degree weather. I have always though it was better to sacrifice the bar, and by doing so save our house and perhaps me.

What I haven't said is Mike and I would often get into fights. He always won and neither of us really got hurt. He was like a cat playing with the captured mouse, except he never went for the kill. One night he did, but it wasn't me he was after, thank God. Mike's mother was away one Saturday night, which was highly unusual. I think it was our senior year and soon the word got out. There were 50 people in Mike's living room, dining room, and kitchen in no time.

People brought beer, the drinking got out of hand, and things started to get broken. I gave Mike a heads up and then said something to someone in the kitchen about winding down the festivities. At this point, someone threw a bottle of beer at me as Mike was coming around the corner from the dining room. He flipped out and started to pick up people and throw them out the kitchen door. The door opened to a small landing which was almost at second floor level. The first one out broke the railing and sailed to the grass below, followed by several others. It didn't take but a few airborne party goers to get the point across that the party was over. In Mike's defense, everyone he threw out was a big guy, but they didn't stand a chance. Mike was uncommonly strong.

A final word about Mike's relationship with cars. At 13 he knew more about them, the engines I mean, than most garage mechanics. His elderly uncle lived with him and his mother for a number of years and had a car in their single detached garage. Mike worked on it all the time, often just taking something apart and putting it back together again. He also knew how to drive at 13 and would take the old tank out for a spin at night.

Mike, with me sometimes, would push the car down the inclined driveway onto the street, which fortunately was also at a slight incline. We would jump in as the car started to roll on the driveway and steer it in reverse down the street a few houses. There it was safe to start the engine and not wake his mother or uncle. Actually, his mother was the only issue, since the uncle was a bit deaf and would not have been stirred by the launch of an ICBM. We would drive around for an hour or so and return by shutting the engine off on the uphill side of the garage, coasting in oh so quietly. We had a huge false sense of security mostly because Mike at 13 looked like he was in his 20s. I think he started to shave at 10.

This was a big deal for me, since I was not a risk taker at that tender age, and I knew if my father found out there would be hell to pay (likely one of the many reasons he thought Mike was not a good influence on me). Mike was not afraid of speed and there for the Grace of God go I.

Lastly a story, which completely contradicts my assertion that Mike was a wonder mechanic. Leslie was given a car one summer when she was a counselor at Camp Beisler. Phil Constantine, the camp caretaker, gave it to her. She was so proud of that car. It was the early 1960s and the car was a classic 1947 Ford. She drove it home and it wasn't running so well. Not surprising since it was over 13 years old and she got it for free. Not to worry, Mike would be happy to fix everything. After working most of the day, things were not much better. In fact, Leslie, to this day, thinks Mike made things worse. The bubble gum just didn't hold up under the heat of the engine. He did his best, but I was crushed, since I suggested he come to the rescue and it didn't work out so well. The car would be a real collector's item today.

6.

VACATIONS

UNTIL LESLIE GOT TOO old to go on vacation with parents, we would take the standard one-week summer vacation. I hated it and was glad she did too (one of the only things we agreed on). We didn't have much money, so it was the economy vacation all the way. The earlier ones were car trips through New England to the usual tourist traps, think Fort Ticonderoga and Frontier Town.

We spent a lot of time in the car, with Leslie and I sharing the back seat. It was like sharing a bedroom, constant skirmishes. I don't know how my parents put up with it. Actually, sometimes they didn't. These trips couldn't have been very restful for my parents, except they were away from 103 Union Avenue, in the wilds of New England.

For some reason we rarely went to a city, say Boston. Maybe because Mom and Dad grew up in the city and wanted more green. There was a loose itinerary, but lodging was not planned ahead. In those days, before there were Holiday Inns in every town, local motels were the venue of choice. Some of these were a bit like the Bates Motel, but it was exciting to me.

While wandering over New England, we would crest a hill and Mom would invariably say "look at the view." I think it was her way of validating the trip. It happened so frequently it became a family joke that Leslie and I still remember so well.

On one of these trips, we made it to Maine and by chance stopped at a place with several small cabins on Brandy Pond in Naples. Our cabin had a sitting area, two small bedrooms, and a kitchenette. We were there for two days and everyone liked it, so Mom and Dad reserved it for a week the following summer. Thankfully, no more car trips. We stayed at Brandy Pond for the following two summers before Leslie became a young adult and vacations ended, thank God.

The cabin was right on the pond, really a small lake. It was great for a family. We rented a boat with a 5 HP outboard and did some fishing, along with swimming, horseshoes, badminton, and tennis. The families got to know one another and some nights there was a cookout, maybe touch football, and a camp fire. Fun for all.

The second summer Leslie had an ear infection and couldn't go in the water. Big crisis, somewhat compensated for by allowing her complete control of the boat. At the end of the week, Dad took me to the boardwalk in Naples and we had an ice cream cone and played the pinball machines. Afterward, we took a walk across the causeway to look at the seaplane, which took tourists on rides in the area. While walking over, Dad said he was happy that I took the lack of access to the boat so well. As a reward, we were going to take a ride on the plane. I was scared and happy at the same time, but it was the best experience I ever had on our many vacations.

7.

Junior High, Bryant School, 7-8ᵗʰ Grades

EXCEPT FOR SOME BRIGHT spots on the playground, the K-6 years at Merritt Memorial were forgettable. At least I would like to forget them, because, as previously mentioned, it was painful much of the time. After 6th grade the kids from Merritt Memorial went across town to Bryant School to join the kids from that side of town, who had been there all along. Keep in mind that Cresskill in those days was only about 3,000 people so the combined 7th grade was small, about 140-150 kids. Nevertheless, this was a big deal, like being in foreign territory. It was made easier because I knew some of the boys from Little League and summer ball. I also could ride my bike and had enough time to come home for lunch.

A word about bike riding, which was my main mode of transportation for many years. I didn't like three speed English Racings. I preferred simple bikes with wide tires and brakes on the peddles. These withstood a lot of punishment. I took after my father in this respect, since I thought all the mechanical stuff on English Racers (hand brakes, and gears to change speeds) were just something that could malfunction. I also thought the fat tires made for a more comfortable ride.

I was pretty good on a bike and often rode with no hands. This caused serious problems two times. The first was when I was in grammar school, coming back from Trip's house after school. I was riding on the concrete sidewalk on a nice residential street. Unfortunately, a large tree root had lifted one of the concrete slabs, converting it into a ramp. I wasn't paying attention, took the ramp, and became airborne. For some reason I blacked out and landed on my head, not breaking the fall with my hands. I was knocked dizzy, but fortunately a girl was walking by and guided me to the doctor's office, which was only about 500 feet away. When Mother arrived and looked at me, she gasped so I knew I was banged up. I recovered.

The second time was strangely similar. I was going to a friend's house riding no-handed when I needed to make a turn down a side street. I could do these turns no-handed, but this time I didn't make the turn sharply enough and hit the far curb. Just like the last time, I went over the handlebars, blacked out, and landed on the sidewalk head first. Also like the last time, I was fortunate in the location, right across from the police station. As I was told later, the cops came running out and took me to the same doctor's office. This time it was two blocks away. When my mother arrived, her gasp was far more dramatic then the first time. I had landed on the right side of my face and scraped much of the skin. I also broke my nose. It took a bit longer to recover. The first few mornings when I woke up, I couldn't open my right eye. It was stuck shut by the fluid from the wounds that had accumulated during the night and solidified in my eye socket. A little warm water fixed the problem, but the first morning it was scary.

Enough about bikes.

During middle school Mom was working for the lawyer Hugh Savoy, so I ate lunch alone. This was fine with me, because on the nicer days, I would inhale a sandwich or two and race back to the basketball court at Bryant School. It was here that I felt most comfortable because I was good, at least in comparison to the rest, and I could make friends and gain respect. We typically played 3 on 3 to 11 points, with the winning team staying on the court for the next challenge. If Rich Ewald and I were on the same team, we usually played the entire lunch break. On hot days I would be drenched and arrive at my first afternoon class in a pool of sweat. Cooling off took a good 15 to 20 minutes, during which time my education was put on hold.

Overall, things in the classroom didn't change much. I was still in the "slow" English class and carried that distinction around like a scarlet letter. There was, however, a significant change on the academic front. In 8th grade my history teacher was Al Monroe. I still couldn't read well and my spelling was worse than atrocious (a word I still can't spell), but I understood the main themes and could connect the dots. For some reason, Mr. Monroe understood this, didn't care about the spelling, and encouraged me to actually be a student. I wasn't ready for it then, but he told my parents at one of those dreadful parent/teacher conferences that I wasn't stupid. This was truly good news for them, although I didn't fully understand it at the time.

The other thing Mr. Monroe did, which helped my self-esteem, was to put me on the yearbook committee. I was one of four, and the other three were some of the best students. I felt a bit, actually a lot, out of place but went along and was grateful for the confidence and trust he put in me. Looking back, it was the beginning of me realizing my potential.

The other big deal during the second year at Bryant was the discovery of girls. My first kiss and hard-on occurred sometime in the 8th grade, but I can't honestly remember the name of the lucky girl. It was most likely Karen Anderson (who was the head of the yearbook committee) or Lynn Mondshein. I was not very comfortable with girls and getting aroused during a kiss, or two or three, made me embarrassed. To compensate, I would often turn a bit sideways to avoid direct contact. It was easier on a sofa, because you were all tied up in knots anyway. Looking back, I guess for 8th grade I did OK, but had no confidence and couldn't understand why any girl would like me. Keep in mind that these encounters were few. Most of the time was spent talking about girls with the boys, although this was mild stuff and not frequent.

One of the hot topics toward the end of our time at Bryant was how far Lenny Lagory got with Julie Marshall. Lenny was a biker type, but at that age it was a bicycle, albeit a very fancy one. He was headed for the Hells Angels. Julie was mildly flamboyant, nice looking, but for 8th grade in all other categories was one step from a Playboy centerfold. Even without Lenny, there would have been discussions about Julie. We couldn't imagine Lenny's good fortune if half of his bragging or gossip were correct. I actually think Julie was much too sensible to have given Lenny free rein, but it was great fun to speculate.

Another good friend during this period was Danny Depolitio. He was a year ahead, but as previously explained we played ball together, mostly baseball and mostly in the summer. Danny's father had lost part of one leg in the WW II invasion of Salerno, Italy. He had a distinctive limp but was held in great respect by us kids as a real war hero.

My favorite memories about Danny were the many hours we played whiffle ball in our backyard. It started just kidding around with a standard whiffle ball and broom stick handle for a bat. Danny was left-handed and could throw a super curveball. It was great practice for me as a left-handed hitter.

We slowly developed a field in the backyard. We had foul lines, lights, and a home plate we stole from one of the ball fields in town (we picked the one that was least used to assuage our conscience). We ran several extension cords from the basement with flood lights and it worked just fine. Night games were terrific, and Mom and Dad encouraged us because it kept us home and out of trouble.

There was a small problem in that the garage, trees, and bushes intruded into fair territory. This was solved by instituting a number of rules about balls that hit things and bounced around. Essentially, we divided the "field" into zones of ever-increasing distance from home plate corresponding to a single, double, etc. It mattered only where the ball landed. You could hit a towering drive, but if it caught a branch and fell in the nearest zone, you only got a single. On defense the most fun was following a well-hit ball as it bounced from one branch to another and softly fell out of a tree into your waiting hands for an OUT. Conversely, a pop flight, usually an easy out, might get hung up in a tree and fall out just beyond your grasp for a base hit.

The rules made for some crazy plays, but things evened out in the end. We had hours of great fun playing whiffle ball. When I played with someone else it never was the same. It needed Danny's spark to make it special.

During the summers after Little League, Danny, Dwight, Sal, Eve Carr, and I played in the Babe Ruth baseball league. There were others, but these were the guys I hung around with, all a year older. We also played golf together, often sneaking on the 11th tee of the local Country Club at 6-6:30 PM. We played until dark and then looked for balls in the water hazards under moonlight. I wasn't any good, partly because I swung the golf clubs like a baseball bat (didn't keep my right arm straight, among other things) and had a terrible slice.

We would take our bikes up to the course and leave them near a hole in the fence where we entered the course. The ride to play was uphill most of the way, and it was a hard ride carrying your clubs. The good news was that after golf, the ride home was all downhill. You could essentially coast the whole way into my backyard.

The only tricky part was timing the traffic light half a block from home so you could sail down the last hill, through the green light at County Road, onto the flat part of Union Avenue and make the turn into our driveway. I did this many times with the golf bag under my arm. One night I missed the driveway going about 30 miles per hour, hit the curb, and took flight along with all the clubs, which shot out of the golf bag like rockets.

I landed on the front lawn and most of the clubs landed in the trees. Amazingly, I kept my wits, landed, and rolled on the soft lawn. I had a few bruises, but no broken bones and the clubs were OK. I needed a new front tire, but considering the speed, it was a happy landing. Not like the two other bad falls when I was younger and blacked out.

Back to baseball. The first year I was in Babe Ruth, most of the other guys my age were still in Little League. It was good for me to get the experience with the older players. It wasn't until the second year when all the guys in my class were in the Babe Ruth league. One, Lynn Farrow, was by far the best pitcher in Little League. He had a high velocity fast ball and decent curve. Lynn would routinely pitch no-hitters, in part because the distance between the mound and home plate was shorter in Little league. His fast ball didn't have any movement, but it didn't matter at the shorter distance. In Babe Ruth, you pitched at the regulation big league distance, 60 feet 6 inches.

There was always the unspoken question of how well I would do against Lynn given that we didn't have much opportunity to play against each other. This changed when he moved to Babe Ruth. Early in the season the team I was on played the team Lynn was on. It was a close game, and I can't remember what I did at my first at-bats. Probably not much, but I can remember the last at-bat.

We were playing at the Bryant School field which had no outfield fence. If a ball got by the outfielder, it rolled on forever. It so happened that I came up in the last inning with the bases loaded and the game tied. I was looking for one of Lynn's fastballs, because it was nice and straight, and I didn't think that hard to hit. He also had good control, so I thought I would get a good one to hit. Sure enough, after a few pitches, I got one right down the middle. I hit a line drive right on the nose just high enough to make it over the right fielder's head. I think he took a step in when the ball was hit and that sealed his fate. A really good outfielder might have caught it, but not that day. Once the ball went over his head it rolled into the next town and I could have walked around the bases. A Grand Slam off the best pitcher in the league, except for Dwight.

Now this completely settled the question of whether I could hit Lynn. I always knew I could, but this was sweet proof. As I crossed the plate our whole team was jumping up and down, as were the few fans present. One was my father, much to my great pleasure. But there was another excited fan, our catcher Hal Watner's mother. Mrs. Watner was a well-known Cresskill force of nature, weighting in at over 300 pounds, much of which was in her well-endowed chest.

I didn't see her moving toward me as I was celebrating with the boys, but as I turned toward her, she gave me a most memorable hug. My head got lost between her two ample jugs and I would have suffocated had she not released me in time. I don't know which was more dramatic, the grand slam or the hug.

At the end of the regular season, a few boys were picked from each team to form an all-star team. Our league covered about six towns, so you got to know a great group of guys outside of your town. It was normally Danny, Dwight, Evey, and me from Cresskill. The team played other teams from around the state for the state champion and ultimately for the national championship, which was played in Oklahoma City.

One year we won the state, middle Atlantic region, and played the New England team for a chance to go to Oklahoma. No one knew how we were going to pay for the trip, but as it turned out we and the season was ended. I didn't start the game against New England, but got up in the late innings in a close game, only to fly out to DEEP right field.

The summer days on the ball field were wonderful.

8.

FRESHMEN AT TENAFLY HIGH SCHOOL

AFTER BEING A HOMESICK kid and terribly afraid of new things, I was about to "go away" to Junior High in neighboring Tenafly and leave Cresskill behind, at least during the day. I was NOT good with change. Cresskill was the "sending" school to Tenafly and, although unspoken, we were viewed as second class students, both socially and financially. Remember, in the 1960s Tenafly was the wealthiest, or close to the wealthiest, town in the country. Cresskill was middle class at best.

We were also going from three classes per day to seven, graduating into the high school system. For a poor student, this was overwhelming, and I had no idea how to handle the change. I also was planning to play football in a new environment, where I knew much less than half of the players. No longer was I going to have any free time to just hang around.

A typical day started early, at least for me, catching the No. 84 bus at 7:30 am. It was a public bus, not a school bus, going to NYC with a stop near the Tenafly Junior High School on its way. It was the same bus many other Cresskill students took, as did my father earlier in the morning. The good news was that the stop in Cresskill for my father and me was just up Union Avenue at the corner. The bad news was that, as a public bus, it didn't wait one extra second if I was late. The trip took about 30 minutes, with several stops, and ended with a short walk to school. On the first day, all the students from Tenafly and Cresskill mingled on the front steps checking everyone out. Very awkward 14-year-olds.

Four classes in the morning, lunch, and three classes in the afternoon. An unimaginable amount of information for me to process (teacher's names, textbooks, locker combination, assignments, etc.). It was clear I was in the slow English class, which was OK with me since I thought it would entail less homework. The bad news, I was in French 1. Although the teacher was young and attractive, I was completely lost from the first day.

When classes ended, the football players had to walk across town to the high school, where the football field, practices fields, and field house were located. The walk was the least of my worries. None of the Cresskill boys had played anything but touch football, without equipment. The boys from Tenafly had grown up in organized Pop Warner football with all the bells and whistles.

Putting on football equipment the first time was like I imagined preparing for a medieval jousting match. It was bulky, heavy, and seemed to do everything possible to limit movement, flexibility, and the ability to use your peripheral vision, an essential tool for any sportsman.

After practice, it was home on the bus without a shower. At 14, that wasn't really a big deal. The bigger problem was carrying all those goddamn books and the thought of homework still ahead. I would get home between 6 and 7 PM, making for a long day, unlike anything I had experienced. Doing this one day was a bit of an adventure, but the thought of doing this five days a week for months, was daunting.

The good news was a hearty meal ready every night, prepared by Mom, followed by halfhearted studying and sleep. Only to be woken to repeat the weekday and yearn for the weekends.

There were times during the first two weeks when I thought I couldn't make it, but routine took over and we found that the Tenafly kids were essentially just like us, only richer.

There were only a few things I remember about the school part of my freshmen year in Tenafly. First, I got a D in French, but learned next to nothing. Going on to French 2 was a lost cause, so Mother suggested I take French 1 again in summer school. More on that later. Second, I got used to the many classes and actually liked the 50-minute limit. The bell was the get-out-of-jail-free card.

By far the most important academic part of my freshmen year was World History class, taught by the Assistant Principal (AP), who's name I sadly forget. Typically, the AP was the school disciplinarian, and this was no exception. No one was going to bullshit this guy. I didn't know it at the time, but I really liked history. My big problems, as already mentioned, were my difficulties reading and writing. Pretty basic problems.

One assignment provided a profound lesson that serves me well to this day. It was given on a Friday for submission on the following Monday. It required writing a 7 to 8-page essay on some topic being studied. At the time it was ancient Rome, and I selected the First Punic War. The Punic Wars were between Rome and Carthage. The first one was essentially a sea battle. Rome won. You will remember the second as the one when Hannibal went over the Alps with his elephants and beat the Romans. That's what you call "turning the flank" and was one of the most audacious military campaigns in history. The Third and decisive war was won by the Romans, Carthage was sacked, and that was the end of that. But I digress.

Picking the topic was easy and fun. As noted, reading the material and writing was a challenge. Sunday, after working much of the afternoon, longer than I had ever worked on a homework assignment, I had a lousy draft and was distraught. I understood the subject but couldn't get it on paper in any coherent way. Mother came to the rescue, as she saw tears in my eyes. She read the mess and help me edit it into something acceptable. She didn't rewrite it, but rather read, with difficulty, a paragraph or two and asked me what I intended to say. As I said it, she made me write it down. I did.

Relieved, I felt better walking into History class Monday morning. Now for the real lesson. Mr. History abruptly stopped us from handing in our masterpieces and said for our Monday night assignment we were to condense/edit the essay to five pages and not lose any of the important content. There was near revolt, which likely would have happened had the teacher not also been the AP.

The process of editing my assignment that Monday night taught me more about writing than anything since. I actually enjoyed it, without my mother's help, and saw how careless I was with words and how much better it read, with essentially the same content. Thank you, Mr. History, wherever you are. Everyone should have the same lesson.

Sports continued to be my only keen interest. I had a bit of a setback in football, given that the golden boy from Tenafly, Danny Wiegert, was the ordained quarterback. I do remember his name. He was about my height with blond hair and movie star looks. The golden girl, also ordained to be head cheerleader, was his girlfriend. I had no chance being the starting quarterback, especially since the coaches knew the boys from Cresskill were not going to be in Tenafly High School the next year, with a new Cresskill High School under construction.

Understanding all this at some level and realizing I was not much better than Danny, I focused on defense. In deference to the coaches, they did play Cresskill kids when there were clear differences in skill. One good example was Mike. As previously mentioned, Mike was a bit mature physically for his age at 6'2," 220 lbs., and strong as an ox. Mike was clearly starting fullback material and won that position as we started the season. More on that later.

Before the season started, I got my big break on defense. After all the exercises and drills, we would often scrimmage at the end of practice. One of the assistant coaches, who was also a math teacher, was over 6 feet, about 250 pounds, none of it flabby, and had huge hairy arms like Popeye, maybe bigger. He had played defense at some college and clearly had an aggressive approach to the game.

One scrimmage, I was playing in the defensive backfield and Popeye was screaming at the defensive linemen to get a quicker start off the ball and penetrate into the offense backfield.

Things were not to his satisfaction, so he walked up behind one of the linemen while the QB was starting to call the play, grabbed the lineman by the shoulder pads with one hand and his ass with the other. As the ball was snapped, he picked up the poor soul a few inches and rocketed him between the offensive guard and tackle at close to the speed of light. When the dust settled, he said good play with a slight grin and the defensive line was never the same again, for the better.

Having a pretty good position to see what was happening, I decided not to be another one of his examples. A few plays later, Mike was given the ball for a run between the left guard and tackle. I saw all this unfolding in what seemed like slow motion as he got the ball and started to accelerate toward the hole. I suspected it would all end in another cloud of dust at the line of scrimmage, since I had the defensive line and the linebackers between Mike and me. It didn't turn out that way. The offensive line performed flawlessly opening a wide hold, and a pulling guard crushed the linebacker. This left only daylight between me and my best friend, both trying to make the starting lineup.

Things seems to remain in slow motion as I saw clearly all this happening. Mike was a step away from full speed and I was flatfooted, the only person between him and the goal line. The physics were not in my favor. Somewhere in my deep instinct to survive I knew I had three choices, all bad. First, I could run the other way and claim I was protecting against the pass. A story that I knew Popeye would laugh at and then proceed to tear me a new asshole. Football career over.

Second, I could go for a high tackle, which with a smaller target might be a good approach. With Mike, it was suicide. The last approach was to dive for his shoelaces and hope he trips over me. At least I'll be in the game even if he scored a touchdown. As history records, I went low, he tripped, and I secured a place on the starting defense. Fortunately, Mike's place as starting fullback was already secured. I also got a nod of approval from Popeye and a physics lesson about leverage.

That brings us to the first game of the season on a late September Saturday morning with Hackensack, a school about twice our size. To start the game at 10 AM, we needed to be at the Tenafly field house before 7 AM. Mike and I took the bus as usual and it was cold early in the morning. Thinking, wrongly, that it would remain cold, Mike kept ALL his clothes on under his pads and uniform. This included the heavy sweater that had been welcomed in the early morning cold. I fortunately didn't do that but did insert a new "cup" to protect my private parts. The cup was larger than normal, which I mistakenly took to mean added protection...also wrong!

As the 10 AM starting time approached, the temperature rose toward an unseasonably high 85 degrees. By the middle of the second half, Mike had lost 10 pounds and was dehydrated and spent. My super cup had rubbed the inside of my legs raw and each step was hell. The second half was a blur and by the end of the game, Mike and I were firmly on the second string. The rest of the season was unforgettable, except, as the season progressed, it became clear to me that I could play QB if I had more game experience.

When football ended, basketball began. I loved basketball, but didn't have much of a jump shot, and like football, almost all my experience was on outdoor courts in 3 on 3 games. Further, I couldn't begin to think of several more winter months of long days and late practices. Once daylight saving's time ended, the trip home was in the dark. I hated that and needed some down time, so I passed on basketball.

During my freshman year I had a growth spurt, up to my full height of 6'1." Strangely, I didn't lose much coordination. One day in November, I was in gym class and we were playing basketball. I got hot, scored some points, and frankly looked good. The basketball coach was watching and afterward came into the locker room and asked me to come out for the team. I said thanks for asking, but for the reasons noted above I passed. I really wasn't that good in my freshman year.

As the weather improved in the early Spring, baseball started. This was where I thought I had the most talent, because, unlike the other sports, I had been playing organized ball since I was 8 years old. I wanted to be a shortstop and as luck would have it, so did Danny Wiegert. In this case, I was better and got the starting spot. One thing the coach especially liked was I hit lefthanded. There were no other lefthanded hitters in our group and most pitchers were righthanded. It also helped that I was clearly better than Danny.

I don't remember much, except I was the starting shortstop all season. There was not much in the way of teaching the game as our coach was not great, and I hated playing in the cold April/May days. These were the days before batting gloves and hitting a ball a bit off center hurt like hell. I also had a low threshold for pain.

By far the best part about playing ball was meeting the guys from Tenafly. Mike and I became friends with Bob Tarsio and John Miller. We were inseparable and fast buddies. Bob was a halfback and John was a fullback, changed to a lineman, because of Mike's talents. Mike was later changed to the line too, but that's another story. There were times during the season when I played QB and Bob and Mike completed the backfield.

Bob and John also played baseball: center field and right field. Mike didn't play baseball. The baseball connection with Bob and John became an instant point of personal pride. Growing up in the New York City area in the 1950-60s included the summer ritual of following one of the three NY teams. Actually, there were only two "real" NY teams. The NY Yankees, at Yankee Stadium located in the Bronx, and the NY Giants, at the Polo Grounds in Manhattan. The third team, the Brooklyn Dodgers, were at Ebbets Field in my hometown Brooklyn. Plenty has already been said about my whole family's affection for "Dem Bums." Of course by 1962, both the Dodgers and the Giants had de-camped to the west coast, but affections remained.

Each team had its center field hero. Mickey Mantle for the Yankees, Willy Mays for the Giants, and Duke Snyder for the Dodgers. Their exploits were made into a catchy tune...Mickey, Willy, and the Duke. Now it just so happened that Bob was a fan of Mickey, John of Willy, and me... guess who. You can imagine the arguments, and they were arguments not discussions, that raged on about who was the best. The war of words often escalated and this was a problem for me as I'll explain later.

In hindsight, after reading many baseball books about the era, it's clear that the Duke was terrific, but not in the same league with Mick and Willy. All three are in the Hall of Fame. Based only on statistics,

Willy may edge out the Mick, but given that Mantle played his entire career plagued by an injury from his first season, I have to give the nod to the Mick. This also takes into account that he was often hungover as the National Anthem began, thanks to his good friends Whitty Ford and Billy Martin. Mick, a young kid from rural Oklahoma (that's redundant), had many other friends in NYC, but too many were bartenders.

This time was truly a golden age for baseball, but I digress again. All fall, winter, and spring during freshman year, Mike, Bob, John and I were always together and payed little attention to the girls. That happened later. Every Friday and Saturday we would gather at Bob's. His father had a successful paving business, and they had a big house. Mrs. Tarsio was the perfect Italian mother. Bob had an older brother and sister, but they were away at school and Mrs. Tarsio liked the kids around. Our place was the finished basement, entered directly from the side door. We were left alone to shoot the shit or play cards. We rarely watched TV. There was also a kitchen well-stocked by Mrs. T. She and our parents liked to know where we were, and we loved it.

Actually, we weren't in the basement much, but in the backyard, where we played football, and the driveway where we played basketball. We would be out there in January in the snow, with the lights on. Mr. T had set up a series of spotlights to allow us to be outside at night. There were often more than the four of us and we had blood games week after week, followed by pizza in the basement. One of Bob's friends, Bob Pieicenta, was a gentle giant a year behind us. He was about 6'3" and 240 lbs. He could bench press some record amount. Bob Tarsio was a smaller version, at about 5'7" 180 lbs. Big Bob was slow. Little Bob was fast. Both were incredibly strong. You didn't want either of them on the other team playing football in the backyard.

One night we started playing basketball and due to my height and speed, I had an advantage over both Bobs. One was too short and the other too slow. After I took advantage of these situations, we would switch to playing football. It got pretty heated and Bob and I would often get into it. He was so much stronger than I, it was no contest. He would get me in a headlock, and I thought I was going to die. This was also, I think, a way of saying "see Mickey is better than the Duke." I quickly raised the white flag, gave up, and would have gone home with my tail between my legs, except that we were such good friends and the pizza was hot.

These friendships were special and made my freshman year a good one.

9.

CRESSKILL HIGH SCHOOL

LESLIE WENT ALL THROUGH Tenafly High and I wanted to continue too, after making it through freshman year with some success and good Tenafly friends. Alas, that was not to be. Cresskill was growing and with the baby boom children coming, Tenafly pulled the plug.

My mother was always in the thick of the school system and was elected to the Board of Education right at the beginning of the planning process for the new Cresskill High School. The Board had some good people including Henry Mazzola, Fred Lyndermyer, Mr. Finch, and Dr. Began, all with kids in the school. Henry was right of Attila the Hun politically, far worse than my father, and my mother was a serious liberal, but they, and the others, got along and got things done. My mother was very smooth and I'm sure outfoxed Henry on many occasions, without him being the wiser. Despite strong personal opinions, decisions were made, and the school was built on time and on budget. Perhaps a lesson for today.

Tenafly didn't give them much time, so a site for the school, with room for expansion, was quickly selected and soon thereafter the brick and mortar phase began. It was a simple one-story building, likely because it was the cheapest and quickest method of construction and the site was large enough to spread out. The ribbon was cut, and we entered in the fall of 1963 as sophomores. The class just before us stayed in Tenafly, so we had the whole place to ourselves and instead of being at the bottom of the pecking order at Tenafly High, we were instantly the "senior" class in little old Cresskill.

This had many implications for the academic and athletic systems. A brand-new school needed a brand-new faculty. The new group of teachers had a range of experience and age, but most were on the younger side. Many newly minted teachers were in their mid-20s, not much older than we were. This turned more interesting as we became juniors and seniors.

I don't have any data to evaluate, but my sense is we had a much better than average group of teachers, and we benefited from this in many ways. Not being a great fan of teachers' unions, I credit the good group of teachers, in part, to the free hand in hiring on merit. Then we were exposed to all the good ones before they burned out. Luck may be the other part.

A school mascot also needed to be picked, so we became the Cresskill Cougars.

I progressed from being in most of the "slow" classes my sophomore year, to being in most of the "advanced" classes my senior year and wonder of wonders, I was inducted into the Honor Society. This happened in part because I learned how to compensate for my dyslexic condition, but also because classes in high school were more focused on understanding content rather than rote reading and writing. I don't think Cresskill was easier than Tenafly, although I have no data to prove that. In any event, I should give some credit to those good teachers who discovered my hidden, very hidden, brilliance.

My first two academic breaks came my sophomore year in Biology and English. Mrs. McConnell was our biology teacher, actually the only one in the school. She lived in town, had two sons a few years younger than we were, and my mother thought highly of her abilities. She was not a rookie teacher and my mother was right about her abilities. I liked biology and it actually made some sense to me. There were systems, great pictures, and explanations about the world around us.

One of the first topics in biology class covered trees and photosynthesis. The simple concept that CO_2 plus water in the presence of sunlight can generate food (organic carbon) and oxygen was fascinating to me. I thought I actually understood the process, but what was really cool was the way trees got water to the leaves, where photosynthesis took place. The tree trunk essentially consists of two key parts, the phloem (bark) and the xylem, all the rest. That meant that except for the bark, all the rest of the tree was essentially a big straw drawing water uphill, through the root system to the branches and leaves above. What seemed solid was actually very porous. For some reason this captured my imagination and opened my mind to how the complex world of nature worked and could be explained to a 15-year-old kid. I studied like crazy, at least for me, and aced a mostly multiple-choice test on trees. Spelling didn't count!

Now that I did it once, there was no reason I couldn't do it again, providing I applied myself. It was a great feeling after years of failure in the classroom.

Next stop, English. Mrs. Clemens was my teacher, with a profile similar to Mrs. McConnell. She was head of the English Department, had a stern bearing and a no-nonsense style. I should have been intimidated by her, but for some unknown reason I wasn't. In the past, English had been mostly spelling, grammar, and long shitty books. To be fair, I was getting a little better about reading. It was still painful, but I was starting to make a little headway. I was training myself to remember certain words that often came up so that I didn't constantly trip over them.

One of the early English topics was Greek and Roman mythology. The Gods were interesting and their relationships and stories fun. The stories were short with lots of pictures and tables. I liked the hierarchy, from Zeus on down and the fact that each had their own specialty. Again, I applied myself preparing for the test and did well. Mostly multiple choice and spelling didn't count, thank God(s).

Actually, there were a few answers that required a short, written explanation. I knew the answers, but butchered the spelling, especially the names of the Gods. In grading the test, Mrs. Clemens took a point or two off for spelling and grammar, but noted a good job and the fact that I clearly understood the subject matter. She cared more about my thoughts than my mechanics. This was a watershed moment that began, along with the biology success, to make me realize that if I applied myself, I could compete with the so-called smart kids.

In junior year I was in the advanced English class, with Miss Pitts. It was her first year, she was young and pretty and I think more uncertain than I was. I was sure I was in over my head and wanted to be invisible in class all year. We took to calling her ZaSu Pitts after a B-grade movie actress, who was a bit flamboyant. Our Miss Pitts was not. She tried really hard with a tough group.

The first day she was going through a roll call to get our names right, including nicknames, a standard routine. ZaSu would call out "Elizabeth Pitkin" and she would say "call me Molly." Before class ZaSu had placed a textbook on each desk. It was about 4 inches thick with thin pages and small print. My heart stopped until I realized it contained 3 novels: Moby Dick, The Scarlet Letter, and Lord Jim.

Restless, I opened the book and saw the famous first line of Moby Dick, "Call me Ishmael." For some reason I could pronounce Ishmael, perhaps because someone in the next row read the line under her breath. In any event, while I was looking at the line, Miss Pitts came to my name and looking around, called out Richard Moore. I promptly blurted out "call me Ishmael" and the class erupted in laughter. Actually, so did ZaSu, much to her credit.

So right off the bat she knew who I was, and my hope of invisibility was lost. Doing something like that and actually pulling it off was completely out of character for me.

One word on high school English literature. If the goal is to get kids to read, which it should be, picking classics like the ones above is a big mistake. I didn't read any of them. For God's sake, Moby Dick has a chapter, a long one, on tying knots. Pick books that are short and have a good story line. Unfortunately, this has not changed and as a result many kids have been driven away from reading, the best pastime ever invented.

As time passed, I slowly graduated to the advanced classes in most everything, except math. Given my later interest in engineering, this may seem odd. Actually, in high school, I was more interested in the non-technical subjects, especially history. At one point, I expected to major in history in college, and except for my complete inability to master foreign languages, I might have.

Don't get me wrong, I was never a great student. I had flashes of brilliance, but mostly I was indifferent, had a short attention span, and cared far more about life outside the classroom than inside.

Two more quick stories before we move on to sports and social life. One happened at the beginning of CHS and one at the end.

We started sophomore year in September 1963, when JFK was president. On the morning of Friday November 22, I was in dreaded French 1, my third try after freshmen year and summer school. I still knew nothing. Miss Cronin, later Mrs. Albanese, was our French teacher. In the middle of the late morning class a messenger came in and whispered something to Miss Cronin. She went white as a sheet, turned, and struggled to tell us that the President had been shot. We did nothing for the rest of the class. Two periods later in the afternoon, during health class, with Mr. Goodwin our football coach and Phys Ed teacher, the notice came that JFK was dead. School was over and we all went home.

This was the Friday before the Thanksgiving week, so that weekend and the next week was wall to wall TV coverage of the assassination, aftermath, and funeral. There weren't many football games on TV in those days, but they were all canceled, including the much-anticipated Army/Navy game. I was naive about the world, but for some reason that cancelation drove home how serious this was for the country, as if anyone needed a sign.

My father was no fan of the Democrats and the Kennedys, particularly Joe Kennedy. I looked to him for signs of how concerned I should be, other than the annoyance of not getting to watch a few football games. He was clearly concerned, but noted much to my relief, that Lyndon Johnson was a solid man and worthy of running the country. Given that Johnson was a Democrat, this was saying something for my father and lessened my concern about the future.

Fast forward to June 1965, the month I graduated from CHS. There were a number of senior events before graduation, including the induction ceremony for the National Honor Society. It included other awards, but I had little understanding of what it was about and no anticipation I would participate in any way.

My mother knew I would be inducted in the Honor Society, which was a big deal for her after sticking by me during all the painful school years. Same for my dad, but he was in the hospital and couldn't attend. More on that later.

I had gone to the Jersey shore the day before with some friends and gotten a terrible sunburn on my back. I tried to get out of the assembly, due to "medical reasons" but my mother would have nothing of it, knowing about the Honor Society. I should have realized something was going to happen, when she made such a big deal about what I should wear to school that day. Finally, I agreed on something reasonable, but I was in agony with the sunburn.

I got inducted, which meant I could wear, along with the other Honor Society kids, the tassel turned to the left side on my motor board at graduation. Mother cried after the assembly, knowing how bad Dad was and that he was not going to be able to attend my graduation. At the time I thought he would be OK and home soon.

Graduation was a big yawn. I had a wonderful time in high school, mostly because of what I'm about to tell you, but I was ready to move on to college and excited about doing so. Before we get to college let's talk about sports and social life at CHS.

Keep in mind that coming back to Cresskill meant we were swimming in a much smaller pool. I could hold my own in Tenafly, but in Cresskill I was at the very top of the sports food chain. This was made more dramatic because we, as sophomores, had no one ahead of us and were essentially seniors for three years. That said, our class had a remarkable good pool of athletes for the size of the school, about 60-70 boys. As it turned out the two classes behind us weren't so lucky and only a few of them helped us in our junior and senior years, and then only in football and baseball.

In New Jersey, there were four groups of schools, based on size. Cresskill was in the smallest, Division 4. Tenafly was in Division 2. Hackensack was in Division 1, the largest. You mostly played similar sized schools, but not always as we shall see.

In our sophomore year we were at a distinct disadvantage, since we had only one grade to draw on to field a team. It wasn't like we were a large Division 1 town and could play Division 4 schools to compensate. Every school we played was bigger than we were, or if the same size had at least three classes to pick players from, with two of the classes older than we were. There was one exception, Emerson. They were a town our size with a new high school and only a sophomore class. These similar conditions naturally created a rivalry that started that first year of 1963-1964.

There were some who took the position that our schools were at an advantage in that we would play together for three years, getting stronger each year. If we could win as sophomores, we'd be that much better as seniors. This of course required a long view, which I decidedly didn't have. My feelings became all too clear in football, where I often found myself on my back under a pile of defensive linemen after a broken pass play, made possible by our clueless offensive line.

Let's look more closely at football. Keep in mind in most high schools, football is the premier sport, followed closely by basketball, with baseball and track a distant third and fourth. I'm not sure why, but likely it's something to do with school spirit. Football starts the school year and gets everyone hopped up. It's also a good way to spend a Friday night or Saturday afternoon in the fall, before the weather gets too bad. Basketball is played inside in much smaller venues where the crowd can really get things fired up. School spirit is used up by spring, when baseball and track come around. Have you ever seen a big crowd and cheerleaders at a high school baseball game? Case closed.

Being the quarterback on the football team is a big deal, but I didn't recognize it for most of my time in high school. First, I was always a good athlete in a small pond and took it for granted that I was to be the QB. I had proven it time and again on the local sand lots for years. Second, at least for the first two years, sports were not a big deal in Cresskill. There was no tradition and honestly, especially as sophomores and juniors, there wasn't much to cheer about.

I also played in the defensive backfield, was the kicker (both punter and place kicker), and received punts and kick-offs. In short, I was always on the field. I was likely better at defense, since I had a good sense of what the other guys were doing. Remember my tackle of Mike as a freshman. I normally was one step ahead of the offense and that helped me make the best of my average speed and strength.

There were times, however, when I guessed wrong. In my last game on Thanksgiving my senior year, I guessed wrong on a key play. I guessed run, and it was a pass over my head for a touchdown. But more often than not, I was in the right spot at the right time and a few of those times I looked like a genius.

My kicking was pretty good too. I kicked the old fashion way, straight on, not soccer style, which was just arriving in football in the 1960s. Starting our sophomore year, Mike was the kicker. He hurt his leg while we were warming up for our first game of the season, actually the first game ever played by a Cresskill High School team. Someone had to step in and kick. I raised my hand and started the game with a kick-off to the 10-yard line. Mike never kicked again.

The next week in practice, I was having trouble reproducing the wonder kicks of the first game. Henry Mazzola often came to our practices, as his son, Kim, was our best lineman. He saw me struggling with no help from the coaches. He came over to offer advice, but first kicked one about 60 yards in his wing tips. I listened. He took his pen and drew a horizontal line about two inches long and 1 inch below the middle of the ball. He said, "Aim for that and see what happens." I did and got my mojo back.

I also inherited the punting in the first game, thanks to Mike's injury. My punting debut was not so impressive. Here too, Henry helped. He pointed out that the key to punting was to drop the ball with the front tip pointed slightly downward and to the left. This allowed the ball to fit into the curve of the upper part of your right foot. If you contact the ball properly, the forward point of the ball will turn upward into a beautiful spiral with great distance. At first pointing the ball downward seemed counterintuitive, but once I got the hang of it, life was good.

Actually, some colleges were interested in my kicking abilities, including Brown -- but they were misguided. I was erratic and soon to be overtaken by the soccer-style kickers.

The highlight of my short kicking career came with a field goal, unusual in high school football, in that Thanksgiving game previously mentioned. It was a beautiful warm November day, but it had been preceded by a week of rain. The field was a muddy quagmire. You were carrying an additional 5 pounds of mud on each shoe and ran in slow motion. As a result, it was a low scoring game with two touchdowns on each side.

I was potentially the goat because I missed the pass coverage that allowed a touchdown in the fourth quarter followed by a 2-point conversion that would have won the game for the bad guys. The score was 15 vs 14 with us on the short end. In the end I kicked a field goal to win the game by 2 points, thus avoiding disgrace and what would have been a difficult Thanksgiving dinner several hours later.

There emerged a different Thanksgiving problem. When my father got back home from the game and turned on the TV to see the noon NY Giants/Detroit Lions NFL game, the picture tube blew up. Doom descended on 103 Union. Fortunately, Mother came to the rescue, as she normally did, and borrowed a TV from our neighbors. Calm had been restored by the time I got home.

Like field goals, a serious passing offence was not typical in high school football. It was mostly 3 yards and a cloud of dust. The running game was easier to execute and there just weren't that many decent quarterbacks and receivers on the run-of-the-mill high school team. A pass was typically a roll-out pass/run option, which often turned into a run. I of course liked to throw the ball and thought we had a few people who could actually catch it. The other consideration was that our running game sucked.

We had a few decent runners. The problem was our line. On paper the offensive line looked formidable: one center, two guards, and two tackles averaging about 220 pounds. Now for a small school, actually any high school, that was a huge line. The problem wasn't size, it was the lack of speed, maneuverability, and the killer instinct. Five nice big teddy bears, who got ripped to shreds by much smaller, vicious opponents. As a comparison, the Tenafly varsity team, when we were freshmen, won the state championship with an offensive line averaging about 180 pounds of raw, mean, explosive power.

If our line couldn't get off the ball quickly, maybe as the theory goes, they could sit still and form a wall to protect the quarterback as part of a passing game. I tried this approach throughout our three years, with mixed results. I was not a pass/run option kind of guy. I dropped straight back into the pocket and hoped for the best. I also called most of the plays, so used the pass liberally, but in hindsight should have used it more.

I had a few games of 200 to 250 yards, which was pretty good for high school; and my total passing yardage senior year was near the top of all the quarterbacks in the county. We never kept good statistics, so I'll never know for sure. The best receivers were Jerry Hilperts, Rich Ewald, and Dennis Ruppert, along with the halfbacks. My favorite plays were the "bomb" and the short pass over the middle.

Many times, I'd throw the ball long and then get immediately flattened without seeing the results. The guy(s) who creamed me was initially thrilled and many times he was justified as the pass fell incomplete. Other times, cheers would accompany a long gain or touchdown. In these cases, the tables were turned, and my proudest moments came as we got up and the defensive guy would look at me and say, "How did you do that?" I was thrilled. There is nothing like your opponent acknowledging your talents.

I was not known for being too kind when passes were dropped, which was often. I'd get pissed, and especially so if the pass went right through the hands of a receiver. At one of our high school reunions, Dennis sheepishly reminded me of the times I took his head off in the huddle after he dropped a pass I thought he should have caught. My reactions were not pretty and probably not called for, at least with the intensity they were delivered. The linemen were also subject to my abuse when they didn't perform. It didn't come off this way, but I was so frustrated because I thought they could do better, if they weren't so lackadaisical.

This brings us to coaching. Now I know it's only a game and we should have fun, but no one really likes to lose. I think we had nice guys as coaches, but they didn't for a minute get the best out of us. The coaching wasn't smart and focused, and it showed. We had never played organized football before and desperately needed coaching. As noted, the best I got was from an interested father. We got some techniques explained, but never the cold steel that makes you play your best and beyond. Winning was just not the culture, and maybe that was OK.

Practices were a good example. They were a bit disorganized, so we didn't make best use of the short time we had. We also weren't physically fit enough to play for 60 minutes. I wasn't the only one to play both ways. There must have been six or eight of us, because we didn't have the depth of talent to draw 22 good players. I also hated getting in shape and that turned out to be a problem and lifelong lesson.

The first game senior year, we were up by 21 points at half time and clearly were outplaying the other guys. In the fourth quarter we just ran out of steam and were killed by sweeps around each end that we couldn't stop because we were too tired. We lost 28-21 and it was because we weren't prepared. I was so upset. I was determined not to be unprepared ever again. If only it were so.

Over three years we won about half of our games and except for a few moments of joy, it was not a distinguished undertaking. I'll end football with a low and high note.

The low point, and it was really low, came our senior year when we played Emerson, our main rival. I don't remember our sophomore and junior year games, as I'm sure they were not memorable, either win or lose. However, going into the senior game, which was away at Emerson, we knew they had a much-improved team based off their record and a little bit of scouting.

We got killed and it was a long afternoon. They were very much improved, well-coached, and out for blood. I couldn't get the passing game going and our lines (offense and defense) were at their worst. We were beaten at every position. I'm not sure I ever wanted a game to be over as much as that one. The only thing I kept thinking about after the game was a chance to play them in basketball. It was a black day for me and the team.

The high point was very personal. It happened one day mid-season during my senior year, after one of those rare 250-yard passing games that we won. I took a shower in the locker room and walked home through little downtown Cresskill. It was a beautiful late fall afternoon and for a brief moment I realized how lucky and blessed I was to have a body in top form and to be able to use it to lead a team, win one for the town, and be recognized for it all. For high school, it couldn't get any better and I was floating along in my own world with these wonderful thoughts. It was close to a spiritual moment and I felt like I could jump over cars, like in the modern day Kung Fu movies. I didn't try, just gave a few parking meters a cuff with my hand like they were good friends I was joking with. Then I got home and life continued in a less rarefied atmosphere. My parents were never ones to suggest that I walked on water. But, if you live 100 years, there aren't too many times you "float," so you remember and cherish them.

There was only a long Thanksgiving weekend between the end of football and the beginning of basketball. Although I think I had less talent in basketball, I liked it best for three simple reasons. First and foremost, we had a good team, only needing five players with one or two backups. A close second was a good coach in Tony Zash, who we liked and respected. Lastly, it was played indoors, where the fans were up close and in your face. I liked the energy from the crowd.

Jerry Hilperts was the center. Not too tall at 6'3," but wide and strong; average speed and decent shot. Rich Kletter was a thin forward at 6'2". He was smart, a good outside shot, average speed, but not as strong on the boards as Jerry. Kim Mazzola was a 6'2" large forward, OK under the boards, and a poor shot. He was also slow.

Richie Ewald and I were the guards. Richie was a perfect guard. Small, fast, good ball handler, and a good shot. I was taller, but mediocre in all other respects. Except at the other end of the court, I was the best defense player on the team because I seemed to have a sixth sense about where the ball was going. I was also tall enough to do some rebounding at each end of the court.

For a small school, this was pretty good talent. Tony was only a few years out of Colby, where he played basketball and baseball. He was also well-known as an exceptional athlete from his days at Englewood HS. He was a small, very fast guard like Richie.

The first day of practice he told us to go to a specific store in Englewood and get a pair of Converse All-stars. We liked him from the start. This was going to be so much better than football coaching. His main job was teaching Spanish, which he didn't much like. He always wore a sport coat with gray slacks, penny loafers, and white socks. We thought the white socks were so cool, until I told Leslie and she set me straight.

Tony knew basketball. He could teach us and show us. He liked a "sluffing" defense and the fast break on offense. We loved it and he pushed us hard to get in shape. He knew we would need to play most of the game and didn't want us to run out of steam, a la football. We ran our asses off while Tony sat on the bench yelling at us. We ran because we didn't want to let him down and we thought we were good enough to WIN. He wasn't Mr. Nice Guy like the football coach. If he got pissed off, he swore like hell and sometimes would play you 1-on-1 and eat your lunch in front of the rest of the team. You didn't want to play Tony, so you ran and ran.

He emphasized defense as much as offense and often made you practice without the ball, which took some getting used to. The idea was to be in position and pass more than dribble. He was an excellent dribbler, with both hands. So, in another drill you could only use your left hand to dribble and shoot. In high school, defenders are not prepared for folks who use both hands. My favorite play was to drive either baseline. On one side you dribbled lefthanded and shot with your right hand, and switched on the other side. Best plays in the book.

However, there were times that the big guys trapped you on the baseline and you couldn't get a shot off. In these cases, a pass to a teammate crossing the paint often resulted in a basket. In fact, passing to a free man for a basket was my biggest contribution to the team. I wasn't the greatest shot in the world, but I did have excellent full court vision and feel for the play. This made passing a natural for me.

Tony loved the fast break and although I wasn't especially fast, I loved it too. It gave me the best chance to show my passing wizardry. The fast break starts with a defensive rebound. The big guy (center or forward) who gets the defensive rebound quickly passes it out to one side or the other. The guards, Richie and me, have already moved to the sides anticipating the pass. One of us gets the out-let pass while the other is headed to the center at mid court. The first guard, say me, gets the out-let pass, turns and immediately passes to the second guard, Richie, who is headed to center court. If that is successful, Richie dribbles to the basket for an easy lay-up. I follow in case Richie misses, in which case I have a second easy chance, while the bad guys are still flatfooted at the other end of the court. Sadly for me, Richie rarely missed a lay-up in these cases.

Things don't always work out so nicely. The bad guys soon wise up. Now, at least one and maybe two of the opposing guards are back defending against the fast break. This actually can make things more fun and rewarding. The classic case works like this. The most troubling defender usually focuses on the leading guard dribbling for the layup.

He is the only one to stop Richie from making an easy 2 points. As they both go for the basket, Richie doesn't shoot, but rather passes the ball behind him to me following close behind for an easy, uncontested 2 points.

There are many variations on this, and it makes for a fun game for the players and fans. There are also a million ways it can go wrong and it's exhausting running at top speed for too long. There was another, unspoken problem with the fast break on our team. Richie, Rich, and Jerry were typically the high scorers, followed by me and Kim. Actually, part of our success was that we all could score, and often there were three or more of us in double figures. That said, there was more than a little competition between Richie and Rich about who had the most points. Jerry was not far behind. Kim and I knew our limitations in the scoring department.

From Rich and Jerry's point of view, every time they started a fast break with an out-let pass was one possession where Richie, or me, had a much higher chance of scoring than they did. Did this cause them on occasion to slow the game down into a more set piece offense, where they had a higher probability of getting a shot and scoring? I'm guessing yes.

To their credit, you often saw Rich and Jerry following closely behind Richie and me on the break, to be in a position to follow up a missed shot.

We had a pretty good sophomore and junior year, considering we were playing bigger schools and older kids. Tony got us a game with Englewood, I'm guessing to knock any chip we had off our shoulders. We were only juniors in a Division 4 school playing seniors in a Division 1 school, noted for their basketball talent. We were crushed and the last quarter was like a Harlem Globetrotters game, and we weren't the Globetrotters.

On a more positive note, we crushed Emerson both years. Our sophomore year we held them to 9 points in the first half and then lost interest. It was bad, but not quite as bad, junior year. They hated us for that so their revenge in football our senior year was understandable.

At the end of our junior year we were in an elimination tournament for the state championship, Division 4. We lost to a team we should have beaten because they turned the tables with their own fast break and just outran us. However, the biggest disappointment was finding out Tony was leaving Cresskill and would not be our coach our senior year, when we thought our hard work would pay off big time.

One last Tony Zash story. As I mentioned, he went to Colby College in Waterville, Maine. He was a very good second baseman and played for several years in the Red Sox farm system, never making it to the Bigs. As you will see in a moment, he was also our baseball coach and good at that too.

Tony's baseball coach at Colby, John Winkin, was well-known and respected in the college ranks. In January our junior year, Tony took three of us to Colby to meet and interview with Winkin. Richie, Rich, and me. Our parents weren't so sure this was a good idea, as they knew Tony better than we did.

One cold Friday we left school a bit early, climbed into Tony's Thunderbird, and headed for Waterville. We didn't have licenses, so Tony did all the driving. We arrived after endless hours, at around 9 that night. Tony pulled up in front of his fraternity house and dropped us off with some half-drunk brother with the instructions to take care of us until Sunday morning, when we were to meet Winkin. As he drove off with little in the way of advice, we stood there in 10-degree weather not knowing whether to be scared shitless or laugh with delight.

This was clearly what our parents were worried about, three inexperienced kids in a den of inequity with no supervision. They were right, because without much ceremony, we dropped our bags in the nearest room, were introduced to two more brothers, and stuffed into a car for a ride downtown. Now, I don't think I have ever seen Waterville, before or since, in the daylight, and that's likely just as well. In the 1960s it was a small, low-income town that came to life on Friday and Saturday nights when the local men came out of the woods to drink, whore, and generally blow off steam. This group of men, tattooed and hardened by the outdoor life in the north woods, were joined by a group of adventurous college guys looking for some of the same sort of entertainment.

So we arrived downtown at Chez Paree, a local strip joint. The women dancing and disrobing on the small stage were not Victoria Secret material, but we watched with our mouths open in nervous wonderment and disbelief. Drinks came, no cash passed hands, at least as we could see, and no one asked for an ID. When we realized it was beer and not soda, we played along like we knew what we were doing, which was not easy since this was our first visit to such a place.

After some time, the natives started cat calling and some tried to climb on the stage and dance. The difference between the woodsmen and college guys was stark. About midnight when things were getting a bit lively, the college guys, at least our guys, understood it was time to go back to the Ivory Towers. We were thrilled when this decision was made.

We were exhausted when we got back to campus, so the first step was to find beds. Their fraternity was three stories with living quarters on the second and third floors. There were small rooms in the middle with desks and closets. Sleeping was done in bunk beds in big L-shaped rooms at the end of each floor. You knew you weren't in Kansas anymore, because these rooms were not heated and the door to the fire escape was left open. Sleeping in any comfort required a heated blanket, which we never got issued.

With many covers it wasn't too bad after you got warmed up, but things got ugly if you turned over, or had to get up and pee. When we told Tony later of our sleeping arrangement, he just laughed and noted that he never had a cold during college and attributed his good luck to the deep freeze.

The next day was Saturday and there happened to be a party planned at the fraternity, as there were at the other five fraternities that night. A party weekend, what we thought was our great good fortune. We helped a bit during the day setting up for the festivities, having never experienced such an event. Further, none of us had ever been drunk, except for a few beers the night before. This was shaping up to be a full-blown initiation, and we didn't know what to expect or how we were going to handle it.

By mid-way through the evening, we were falling over drunk, blew lunch (and dinner) in the snowbanks behind the house, and gamely went back to dance to the band in the basement. The basement probably had a safe capacity of 40 people and there were at least 100 drunk and crazy people dancing to the music like one connected mass of protoplasm. You didn't have to ask anyone to dance. Once you hit the basement floor, you were swept up in the moment. We were in heaven, beyond our wildest dreams.

I'm not sure how we made it through the night still standing, but we did. We didn't stick together so we each had different experiences and more importantly no witnesses to our individual bad behavior. As I recall, around 2 am when things had died down and most had gone to bed, Richie and I were sitting in the first floor trying to decide if we should throw up one more time before going to bed in the deep freeze.

A few guys were also hanging around reliving the evening's highlights, when one guy told an interesting story. Apparently in the basement there were times during slow songs, when couples actually danced together. One guy in a deep embrace, all of a sudden lost his cookies, in a replay of Vesuvius, all over his date. He then fell dead drunk and unconscious on the floor.

The lovely co-ed was none too pleased, as you might imagine. As the other dancers parted and the music stopped, she proceeded to strip the shirt off the guy and turn him on his back. She dropped trough, squatted, and dropped a stick (shit) on his chest. As it was told, she was cheered during and after the act. Now, none of us could verify this story, but we were still laughing when we hit the deep freeze.

Sunday morning was not kind. We had to meet Tony and Winkin in the cafeteria at 10 am for an "interview." We struggled to get there on time, filled our trays, sat down, and couldn't look at the food. We were all a wreck and I remember nothing of the interview. We left about noon for the long drive home. Not much was said as we nursed headaches and nausea all the way.

Many years later, I was talking to Kim about our time with Tony. His father, Henry, as President of the Board of Education, knew all the dirt in town. Henry apparently liked to be in the know, a little like J. Edgar Hoover. In any event he had told Kim that Tony left at the end of our junior year in large part because he was screwing the school nurse and got caught. He also happened to be married. He apparently took us to Colby, not so we could interview with Winkin, but because he had an old girlfriend in Waterville who he wanted to spend the weekend with. Whatever the reason, it was a memorable trip for three 16-year-olds.

As I mentioned, we had great expectations for our senior year of basketball. The problem was we were undisciplined, a problem Tony could solve by being a hard-ass son-of-a-bitch. Unfortunately, our new coach, Al Goldman, could not. Where Tony would scream and swear at us and teach us new terrible words, Al didn't swear. The worst it got was after one particularly bad practice he exploded with "you guys were piss-poor." We were shocked.

Speaking of new words, Tony introduced us to two wonderful ones. Both came up while he was talking, more likely screaming, at us in some locker room. They were flatulence and defecation, or as it first came up, "you were defecated all over." We loved those words because they were both somewhat sophisticated and naughty, and weren't banned. You could actually say them in mixed company (with parents present) and not get your head taken off. Might even get a slight smile from a knowing parent. Of course these were "big" words, so it took some time using them among ourselves before being confident enough to use them elsewhere.

One day in the locker room we were complaining about all the running we were doing. Tony jumped in and said "If you don't like it, go home and screw your girlfriend." According to him, one 'active' hour in the sack equaled 20 wind sprints. Our mouths dropped open, as we had never been in the "sack." Tony was memorable!

Al Goodman was a really nice guy, but not a basketball genius, and because he was so nice, didn't gain our respect. Tony taught us important stuff, especially how to play defense (one hand up and one hand down), had game plans, and adjusted them as he saw the strengths and weaknesses of the other team as the game progressed. Al tried to do this, but compared to Tony, it was a weak performance.

As a result, we reverted to the type of game we grew up with...3 on 3 with all the emphasis on scoring and not defense. Our game plan, as described by one of the Richards, was for the first guy with the ball across half court to shoot. This didn't lead to a team effort and the results showed. We had a good record but lost several games because we had no direction going down the stretch. Tony would have given us that.

We did get off to a good start with a win against an OK team. Just so happened that I had more rebounds than anyone else, as a guard. This was pointed out by Al and really pissed off the "big boys." They were determined that this not happen again and was a good motivator, at least for a few games.

Over Christmas we were in a tournament with three other teams. There were two games the first night and the winners would play the next night for the championship. The losers would play a consultation game. We won our first game, likely the best I ever played. I had 22 points in the first half and was white hot. The only problem was that my excitement caused me to accumulate many fouls, playing defense at the other end of the court. A good coach would have pointed this out and calmed me down. Unfortunately, this didn't happen and with about a minute left to play in the first half, I fouled out! In the locker room at half time, I was sitting there and realized I wasn't going to play in the second half. I was not used to being a spectator. It was the first and only time that happened, to me or anyone else on the team.

At least we won and would be in the final game the next night. Rich knew one of the guys on the other team we were to play. He had played with him the previous summer and had been talking about how good he was for several weeks before the tournament. Rich made him out to be some kind of super star, who we couldn't begin to stop. We were intimidated. After our win we watched him play in the second game and indeed he was good. He was also a lefty, and as I previously noted, that worked much to his advantage.

The next night, once we started the championship game, it became clear that although good, the guy could be stopped. I focused on that with some success, although he did score a lot of points. Fortunately, there were no other super stars on their team, and we battled them evenly all night. I had lost my hot hand from the night before, but others kept us in the game.

We were up by one point with less than 10 seconds left when Kim fouled one of their guys in the back court, not a good play. The guy made the two free throws and they won the game. It was a great game, but we lost. I remember saying in the locker room at half time that we could beat these guys... they were not super stars. The coach should have been saying that, not me. Again, better coaching could have made the difference. Tony would have never let us think we were going to be outclassed. It was a painful but good lesson about not overestimating the opposition, without good cause.

Fast forward to the state tournament in March. We won our first three games, including beating the team we lost to the previous year quite convincingly. This brought us great joy and to the semi-final game with a team from south Jersey we had not played before. Like the Christmas tournament, we played even until the end. They were ahead by one point and we had the ball at mid court, with a few seconds to play.

Coach called a time out to organize our last play, which was a good move on his part. Unfortunately, in our huddle he instructed Kim to throw the ball in play, and to throw it to me of all people. With Kim throwing the ball in, I was the worst shouter on the floor, so this made no sense to me. Coach wanted me to dribble to the basket and take a shot, presumably with the hope of making it or being fouled. Why he picked me will forever be a mystery, but perhaps he knew from football that I could deliver in the clutch, despite the fact that this was basketball, not football.

We executed the first part, but I was doubled teamed and couldn't get a shot off. I passed to a free man, can't remember who it was. At the buzzer a shot was taken and missed. We lost by one point. Sad day in Muddville, but there was a silver lining of sorts.

Right after our game was the other semi-final game. We sat in the stands with the team that had just beaten us to watch the game and see who they were going to play the next night. We joked with the other guys, shared our take on the game we played, and had some fun. As the other game progressed, it became lopsided as one team completely outplayed the other. The better team was clearly outstanding in all aspects of the game and you could see how intense and focused they were. By the end of the game, we wished our new friends luck, but you could see in their eyes that they wished, at some level, that I had made that last minute shot a few hours earlier. The next night we went to the finals. It wasn't pretty. Our friends lost big and we were happy to be sitting that one out.

We ended the season on a reasonably high note, playing hard to the final buzzer in some exciting games. During the season, we actually won a few of the close ones. And we beat Emerson, although it was way too close. For some reason we were all "cold" that night, despite the revenge we wanted for the football defeat. Rich was the only one who didn't taste that bitter football pill.

On another level, we all thought we didn't play up to our potential because of the lack of strong coaching. I especially felt this way, although I'm not sure Red Auerbach could have help us win against the team that won the state championship. So for me the season highlight was a very personal development, which strangely had a connection to football.

Thanks, or no thanks, to our offensive line, I got my share of bumps and bruises on broken pass plays during the football season. As I have mentioned, this prompted many angry verbal responses from me. Despite this, the linemen tried hard to protect me. I knew it and they knew I knew it. In a small way of tipping their hat to me, the group would come to the basketball games and cheer me on. During one early game our senior year, one of the guys, I think Jason Carl, bellowed out my name after I scored. He took the liberty to shorten it to RMoore. The next time he modified it to extend the R about 3 seconds followed by a resounding Moore. The rest joined in and as it was perfected, the R started softly and rose in volume to a peak, followed by a deep, sharp Moore.

In short, the boys-of-the-offensive-line developed a cheer especially for me. I never recognized it while playing, but I was proud of it and cherished the gesture. Now, it's common for players to say that they don't hear specific things yelled by individual fans during a game, only the background noise. This is not completely true. I often heard the RMoore cheer, but more to the point, I heard my father when he wanted me to.

Good old Henry Mazzola and my father would come to as many games as possible. Both had played and both knew the game. When we were doing something stupid, or playing badly, my father would make a pointed suggestion. And he would not speak softly. Now this didn't happen often, but when it did, I heard the message.

Another message I got from my father came during the basketball season my junior year. I was taking math with Dick Sharry and I had a rough patch with a test or two. Since this grade was considered important for college admissions, Mr. Sharry wisely mentioned this to my dad and suggested some sort of wake-up call. My father immediately, or as they say "in a New York minute," took me off the basketball team. This got my attention, my grades improved, and basketball resumed. A classic case of tough love, properly applied.

Now, on to springtime and baseball. The baseball season wasn't as much fun as football and basketball because, as mentioned, no one came to the games except a few parents. Fans make it fun, and to make matters worse, the baseball field was as far away from the school as you could get while still being on school property. No one passed by and no one knew we were playing.

Also, like in basketball, Tony wasn't our coach senior year. But, before he left, he taught us a few useful things. As I mentioned Tony wasn't a big man, but had great wrists, a la Hank Aaron, and could use them to get a great deal of bat speed. He was a line drive hitter and taught us to hit 'down' on the ball. This was good for me, because I had a big 'upper cut' swing trying to always hit a home run. Hitting down on the ball helped me to flatten my swing with good success.

At practice one day I was playing shortstop and missed a ground ball. Tony came wandering by as I was hanging my head. He knowingly asked if I knew how to catch a ground ball, being a very good retired second basemen. I looked puzzled and he said it was easy. Just squat down like you are taking a shit in the woods. I tried it and it worked, although I had never taken a shit in the woods and was guessing at the technique.

Not having Tony as our coach was a bummer, but at least we had a guy, Ed Bauer, who was also a good ball player and knew something about the game. The only problem was that Ed didn't talk very much, so his advice was difficult to extract. He was also the driver's ed. instructor and let me — actually encouraged me — to skip lessons. I got my driving certificate without once getting behind the wheel.

The senior season started off with a bad thing and a really bad thing. First, our star pitcher, Lynn Farrow, decided he wanted to play golf, not baseball. I tried my best to shame him into playing, with no luck. This meant I had to pitch, and this was not a good thing for anyone.

My best position was catching, but I didn't like squatting all the time. This was a big mistake, since next to the pitcher, the catcher is the most important defensive player. I wanted to play shortstop and since I was perhaps the best player at any position, I got to play shortstop and, thanks to Lynn, pitch too.

The really bad thing occurred during our first game against Fort Lee. Since Fort Lee is at the NJ side of the George Washington bridge, it was easy for my father to attend. He just got off the bus from NYC a few stops early. As was the case in basketball, he met Henry Mazzola at the game.

The basketball team was well-represented on the diamond. Richie Ewald played centerfield and batted lead-off. I batted third and Kim Mazzola played third base and batted fourth. Richie was a good lead-off hitter, usually getting the bat on the ball and he was a fast base runner. I was a pretty good hitter for power and average. Kim could hit the shit out of the ball but struck out a lot and was slow on the bases.

Fort Lee had a nice field with a short right field fence. Right behind the fence was the school auditorium with huge windows. I couldn't help but notice this warming up. Being a lefthanded hitter, I was thinking about breaking one, or more, of those big windows.

The first time I got up, I hit the ball about as well as I could, but it was a line drive right at the right fielder. A little higher and surely a window, but it was not to be. The right fielder caught the ball on one bounce without moving. I hadn't taken a step out of the batter's box, having hit the ball right on the nose. The right fielder, from habit I guess, started to throw the ball into the second baseman. As he was doing this I started to run, with the slow realization that if he changed his mind, he could throw me out at first base.

Fortunately, his thinking was a bit too late and he continued his throw to second base. I was running like hell by now, realizing my vulnerability. My father had arrived and also pointed that out, at the top of his lungs. The shortstop, who was receiving the throw from right field, also understood what was happening, as now everyone did. He got the ball and immediately threw it to first base, a second too late. I was safe but didn't get any further and shortly the inning was over. At least I didn't embarrass myself by being thrown out at first from right field.

I was pitching and we lost by one run. We could have used Lynn, and I never got close to those windows again. I also never heard more pointed advice from my father, although I could have used some. After the game we were walking to the bus and Henry pulled me aside. He explained as matter-of-factly as possible, that my father had passed out when he was yelling some advice, perhaps during that first inning, I'll never know. An ambulance had been called and he was taken to the hospital for observation. Henry was sure it was nothing serious.

By the time I got home, so was my father, resting in bed. He looked a bit washed out and was going to the doctor for more tests in the morning. This was going to be the first time my father missed a day of work and the first time he had seen a doctor since he was in the Navy. He was 56.

The rest of the season was uneventful, save for four memories, as told in order of importance. First, we beat Emerson twice. Second, in one game, Rich, Kim, and I hit triples in the first inning. All together we scored 5 runs in that first inning and, despite my pitching, held on and won the game.

Even though we were a small Division 4 school we were scheduled to play Hackensack, Division 1 and Tenafly, Division 2. I pitched both games. We lost to Hackensack by two runs after Rich let a line drive (like my hit against Fort Lee) go through his legs in center field and roll to North Carolina. That was OK, shit happens, but my real frustration was my hitting.

The Hackensack pitcher was a lefty who threw a lot of big round-house curves. I actually loved these because I had so much practice hitting the same pitch from Danny, both whiffle balls and hard balls. Sadly, that day in Hackensack, I could only hit long foul balls and never got a good one fair. I too could have reached North Carolina.

The highlight of the season came against Tenafly at home. Bob and John were on the Tenafly team, which made it all the more personal. Mr. Tarsio came to the game and my father would have been there, but for the fact that he was in the hospital. Mr. Tarsio and my Dad would have had a wonderful time bantering back and forth as the game proceeded, but it was not to be.

Bob was a terrific hitter, batted third, and was by far Tenafly's most dangerous player. I wasn't about to give him a good pitch to hit. I walked him the first two times, not intentionally, but for all practical purposes that's what it was. We scored a run or two, I can't remember how. As Bob came up the third time, and likely his last, since we only played 7 innings. He was clearly frustrated and knew exactly what I was doing. His father knew too and was yelling for me to pitch to him. Not on your life. I gave him nothing good to hit and he walked for the third time. He was pissed, but we won the game and he knew he would have done the same thing in my position. Tony would have loved it. I actually used my head.

The baseball season was a bummer right up to graduation, since shortly after the Fort Lee game, my father was diagnosed with lung cancer. About two weeks after the game, he was to be admitted to a hospital in NYC. The day he left, we sat on the back porch and he said I was now the man of the house while he was gone. I don't know if he knew how bad things were, but my guess is he did. He didn't let on for a minute that he might not be coming home, and it never crossed my mind.

For the rest of the school year, my mother went to see him almost every day/night and I went often, but not often enough. Both my mother and father wanted me to enjoy the last few months of high school, as there was so much going on. I never thought that he wasn't going to get better, once the doctors took the cancerous part of his lungs out.

I was completely naive about this, maybe because I wanted to be, as the alternative was too painful to contemplate. Right before graduation they operated, and I saw him a day or so after. While I was growing up, we used to arm wrestle. Dad always won. I was a kid and he had big strong hands. It was his way of saying that he was still the boss and I shouldn't get too cocky.

We hadn't done any arm stuff in some time when I saw him in the hospital. Mom told me he was very weak after a major operation, so not to be upset. When I saw him, he was a shell of his former self. This seemed to happen so fast, but I figured he would slowly gain his strength and we would be back to arm wrestling.

As we were saying goodbye, he lifted up his right hand, bent at the elbow, as a way of shaking my hand while saying good luck at graduation. When I took his hand, there was nothing there. I mustered all my willpower to be positive, but I was shaken. I should have realized things were very bad but couldn't face the reality. Graduation was a hollow event, bravely attended by my mother and Leslie.

Through all the classroom stuff and sports, my social skills began to develop, although it was a rocky road. This was a classic case of the outside me versus the inside me. From the outside, I should have been a "Master of the Universe" in Tom Wolf's words. I overcame my academic insecurities, at least in part, and I was the star athlete. I was the quarterback on the football team and picked for the All Bergen-Passaic County All Star Basketball Team. I was also captain of the baseball team. I was picked as most athletic for our yearbook and some years later, elected to the Cresskill High School Athletic Hall of Fame. I was a good high school athlete, and in a small school had many opportunities to show my stuff.

A word about the basketball honor. Keep in mind Bergan and Passaic counties had some of the best basketball in the country in the 1960s. Some players went on to the NBA, and more would have, but for jail. The only reason I made the team was Henry Mazzola. He was a newspaper guy and knew all the sport writers. He lobbied for me, called in some favors, and I got the nod. Thank you, Henry.

Given all this sport stuff, I should have been able to walk on water, at least socially speaking. But high school is a tricky place socially. In short, I wasn't cool. Too straight and conservative at a time when James Dean was hero to the young. Also the inside me was hugely insecure socially, and I'm sure it showed. My biggest hang-up by far was my skin problems. I had acne and it colored absolutely everything I did socially.

I was tall and not ugly, but the acne thing killed my confidence like a spike in the heart. This kept me out of the social scene during my sophomore and junior years, except for a few dances. Girls would normally say yes if I asked them to a dance, since, at least on paper, I was considered a good catch. But I was so uncomfortable, mostly due to the acne, and since my only form of transportation was my bike, things were dreadfully awkward.

Diana Angelettie, a hot, very hot sophomore, accepted my invitation to the Junior Prom, but she had no interest in me, and I had no idea what I was doing. It was a set piece boor.

This all changed the summer before my senior year. But before we get to that summer, a word about the previous summer. As you would expect, there was pressure from my parents to make some money during the summer, especially after sophomore year. My solution was to cut grass in town, something I had done a bit the previous year, but now I planned to expand my customer base.

Since I thought I would have more work than I could handle, I asked Mike to be my business partner. However, after I exhausted family friends and acquaintances, the pickings were slim and Mike wasn't much help on the new business side. He also slept until noon and getting him to the job site in the morning was a challenge. I didn't mind at first, because we didn't have much work and I could easily do it and collect all the money.

Then one day while I was cutting a lawn, the woman living next door came over to ask if I would be willing to do a landscaping job in their backyard. I had no idea what she meant, but of course said yes. Turns out their backyard was about 100 feet wide and flat for about 30 feet from the house. Then the land rose in an incline for another 30 to 40 feet at about a 3 to 1 slope. This meant the top of the slope was about 10-12 feet higher than the flat part of the yard. At the top of the slope the land flattened out into the backyard of the next house.

The flat part of the yard was covered with grass and looked nice. The sloped area was a mess, with clumps of crabgrass, weeds, and small shoots that wanted to be trees. She wanted us (I told her about my partner) to clear the slope and rake the dirt smooth so the folks from the local nursery could come in and replant the area.

This didn't look like a big job, but I had no idea how much to charge. She said that I should come back early the next morning to negotiate a price with her husband, before he left for work. I was thrilled and stopped by Mike's on the way home to tell him the good news and to be ready the next morning to tackle "the hill." At home that night I told the story to my parents at dinner, and they agreed charging by the hour would be the best approach.

The next morning, bright and early, I went to Mike's and found him fast asleep. His mother worked for the post office and went to work at 4:30 am, so she was never there in the morning. I just walked in, went upstairs, and tried to get Mike going. Mike was dead to the world and no amount of reasoning or screaming had any impact. With time running out, I finally went to negotiate the hill work.

The husband wanted no part of an hourly rate agreement, pointing out correctly, that we could milk the job all summer. Although I protested and promised efficiency, he wanted a lump sum. I was intimidated, backed down, and agreed. I woefully underestimated the work and settled on a price that sounded to me like a lot of money, but was, for him, a steal.

I started the work and quickly understood how bad a deal I made. By lunch time I did a quick calculation and realized it would take three times as long as I anticipated. Ripping one clump of weeds at a time was backbreaking work in hot weather with no shade, and I had brought the wrong tools. The tool issue was partly solved when the wife allowed me to use the tools they had in their garage, but I needed Mike for his power and company.

By the end of a long, lonely day, I was exhausted. On the way home I stopped at Mike's and told him the story, but not the whole story. I stressed his cut of the money and how I needed his help. He assured me things would be different the next day. When I got home and told the story in more detail to my parents, I must admit I was looking for a way to get out of the deal. No chance, a deal is a deal, even if you made a bad one. Suck it up and get it done. I had a reputation to uphold.

The next morning, with aching muscles and blisters, I arrived at Mike's and found the same situation. I didn't have time limitations since I didn't need to meet anyone at the house to start work and I was determined to get Mike to do his duty.

I had no luck in the bedroom as Mike was dead to the world again, so I sat in the corner considering my next move. I picked a specific place because Mike had dozens of girly magazines in his room. These were cheap versions of Playboy that his mother took from the post office apparently because they were returned. I never was clear how she got them but enjoyed the result.

As I sat there leafing through the mags, I was getting hungry. I told Mike that I would buy him breakfast if he got up. No luck, so I said I was going to the kitchen to make breakfast. I found eggs, bacon, and bread, turned on the burners and began to cook. The smell of bacon was too much for Mike and he showed up in the kitchen as I was finishing breakfast.

I told him to sit down, I would feed him, and then we would go to work. I had just finished two eggs, he finished the other 10 along with the entire loaf of bread, less my two pieces. By the time he was finished I had also cooked the ½ pound of bacon, again less my three pieces. I knew Mike had a big appetite, but I was amazed at his performance.

For the next two weeks we did the same thing almost every morning. He missed one or two. We finished the hill job and both made a few bucks, but the hourly rate was way, way below minimum wage. Lots of sweat and blood and maybe a good lesson in cost estimating and negotiating.

At the end of my junior year, there were two big family events in the same June weekend. Leslie got married to Henry Brubaker, a fine Dutchman from Lancaster, Pennsylvania, and graduated from college, in that order. She had met Henry the summer before at the Jersey Shore and the deal was struck over Leslie's senior year at Cedar Crest and Henry's year at Lehigh, while getting his master's degree in political science. As the story goes, Mom and Dad offered to pay for a big wedding or give them the money and have a small one. Wisely, they took the money. Apparently, this was not Mother's wish, one of the few times she didn't negotiate a successful outcome.

In those days, the women's movement had not fired up and college was a good place for a young woman to find a husband. In Leslie's case she did just that, and found a good one. She and Henry were married on the Friday before her Sunday graduation from Cedar Crest. This meant that at graduation she was announced as Leslie Moore Brubaker, a clear statement to the rest of the class that she was hooked. I was sitting next to Dad at the sunny, outdoor ceremony and as Leslie was walking off the podium, he leaned over to me and said "$10 grand, shot to hell." He said it half in jest, as I believe he thought the investment in college was to be used to get a job, not a husband. Leslie did just fine and I think deep down Dad thought so too. Henry was worth every bit of the investment.

10.

CAMP BEISLER, 1964

THE IDEA OF REPEATING the summer on "the hill" was not to appealing to me, and Mike as a partner was not in the cards. It so happened that Leslie had worked at a summer camp, as a counselor, a few summers previously. She got the job through the Lutheran church we attended, perhaps with some influence by Mom. It was the Lutheran camp for New Jersey, Camp Beisler, and Mom suggested I give it a try. I guess Leslie hadn't pissed anyone off because I got a job on the maintenance staff. I was a bit too young to be a counselor and actually I preferred not having to deal with the lovely little campers.

I had mixed feelings about going away the summer before my senior year. On the one hand, I wanted to leave Cresskill, but on the other, I was very concerned about being homesick. My parents encouraged me to take the job, even though it only paid 25 dollars a week, yes that's per week (less than the hill work). At least they fed you three squares per day. I suspect in hindsight my parents thought the experience of being away was more important than the money. Wise folks.

The staff arrived at camp one week before the first campers to get things ready after the winter. Phil and Ellen Constantine were the caretakers, who lived year-round at the camp in a beautiful old stone house with their two young kids. There was a much newer main lodge next to the stone house which was kept open all winter for small retreats of no more than about 20 people. During the off-season, Phil and Ellen managed the retreats. Phil was the cook.

The rest of the camp was closed for the winter. In that first week we opened the cabins, mess hall, infirmary, bathrooms, and arts and crafts buildings. There were three of us on the maintenance staff working for Phil: Carl, Bob, and me. Carl had been there the previous year, so he was first among equals. Bob and I were first timers. I liked Phil a lot and Carl was a good guy, not taking advantage of his seniority, at least not too much. Bob was a prima donna, which was obvious from the start. He was tall and good looking, and thought he was a hot shit. My initial concern was that he wasn't going to be a hard worker.

As usual in a new situation, I was concerned I was going to do something stupid and make a fool of myself. Plus, I was completely naïve, and was unsure of how to do the simplest things. Do you leave your toothbrush in the head or take it back to your room? Things like that.

The maintenance, kitchen, waterfront and admin staff lived in the lodge. The counselors lived in the cabins with the campers. Our living arrangement, compared to the counselors, was like the Ritz compared to a Motel 8. Our rooms in the lodge were on the second floor: the right side for the guys and the left side for the ladies. There were six or seven guys in four rooms, so there were two to a room.

I roomed with Bob and we all used the bathroom at the end of the hall. There were only three girls on the other side, so they had plenty of room. We all ate our meals in the mess hall at a prescribed time. Each table had 12 seats. During the first week, all the staff sat at a few tables. Once the campers came, each table had 10 campers and two staff. I was on time for lunch and dinner, but had a hard time making breakfast on time. I took a lot of shit for being late from the counselor I was assigned to sit with. She was pissed I could get a bit more sleep then she could.

During the first week, the maintenance staff worked hard getting things ready. We had to clean the cabins and outfit them with bedding, something the counselors helped with, and a million other tasks.

Turning on the water, cutting grass, getting the heads operational (boys and girls), and cutting piles of wood for the opening campfires.

After a few days, Phil said we were going to paint the main buildings (heads, mess hall, infirmary, arts and crafts building). These were big buildings and we were going to spray-paint them. Using a paint brush and roller would have taken years. The spray system had a 10-gallon reservoir for the paint, two long hoses, one for the paint and one for the compressed air, and a small gas engine to supply the air pressure. The two hoses were attached to a spray gun that you held, aimed at the building, and pulled the trigger.

Getting this all to work correctly from the top of a ladder wasn't so simple. But when it did work you could get a lot done quickly. Since this was the shittiest job, I got nominated to paint the first building, the head. The main head had a boys' side and a girls' side with toilets and showers and was a large building. It took me some time, all morning, to get the hang of all the equipment working together. Phil came to inspect just before lunch and was none too pleased with my lack of progress. He mumbled something about getting the building all painted in two days, and I had already used up 25% of the time with little to show for it.

After lunch things went smoothly and I finished the building by mid-afternoon of the second day. Phil was impressed. That was the good news. The bad news was I "won" the role of head painter for the rest of the buildings. I really didn't mind this because now I knew what I was doing, and I was good at it. Unfortunately, there were two things I hadn't anticipated.

First, I got a terrible head cold. My sinuses were completely clogged, I couldn't sleep, and when I did, I woke up with my eyes sealed shut with dried fluid. It was terrible, but I couldn't let Phil down, so I kept working and didn't tell anyone. By the second day, I had developed a fever, but still didn't tell the nurse. The next night I had hallucinations and dreamed I had gotten up and gone to the bathroom to pee. After I finished the pee, I realized I was still in bed. This was humiliating and I tried to cover it up, with little success.

I went back to work not knowing if I was going to make it through the day. It was another day of spray-painting. When the wind was blowing in the wrong direction, you ingested a good portion of the paint. I should have worn a mask, since it was lead-based paint, but this was long before OSHA. Going up the ladder one time, I scraped my hand against one of the rungs and broke open a scab on the base on my hand. It had been a good-sized cut and it bled quite a bit. It soon sealed up as the mixture of blood and paint dried up, and I went on painting.

It was another difficult night, but at least I didn't pee in my bed. However, in the morning I had a bright red line about ¼-inch wide heading from the cut on my left hand up my arm, approaching my shoulder. I also couldn't open my teeth more than about ½ inch. I had blood poisoning and lockjaw!

I walked into the mess hall looking like shit, and approached Nurse Joan. As I showed her my arm, the rest of the breakfast table gasped. Joan was a tough cookie, didn't look concerned, and suggested I have something to eat and meet her at the infirmary after breakfast. Most of the table thought she was crazy, but I was hungry, so I sat down and didn't make a fuss.

Eating was a bit of a trial given the small space between my teeth. I did my best to stuff in some food and proceeded to the infirmary. Joan lanced the wound, which was under considerable pressure, and the bad fluids rushed out. This was followed by a tetanus shot, a bandage, and back to painting. That day the fever broke and the lockjaw subsided, as did the cold. It had been a trial by fire over several days and I had passed.

It was a horrible week, but by the end Phil and I had forged a lifelong bond. When my parents came to have lunch with me on Saturday, I was not good company, but told them nothing of the weeks' bad events and, although sad to see them go, I stayed.

If I was still homesick after one week, I wasn't after two. You see, the campers came the second week.

In my mind's eye, I saw campers as cute little 8-year-olds. I hadn't anticipated that the oldest campers would be only a year or two younger than me, and mostly girls. I was clueless, but Bob wasn't and quickly started to size up the group of older girls at the opening campfire. My first reaction, as usual, was to keep a low profile. I also wasn't 100%, still recovering from the cold, fever, and blood poisoning.

There were of course a mix of boys and girls (men and women) on the staff, and there were opportunities for staff romances. I was likely the youngest staff member and romance was the last thing I was thinking about that first week of camp.

Actually, Leslie had a fling with Walter Blue when they both were counselors. Walter was still at camp when I arrived but had been promoted to Assistant Director. He was quite a character. Great with the campers and very artistic. When we would be riding in a car passing a farm, he would have us hold our breath until we counted all the cows. One of the many crazy but fun things he did.

We had an early opportunity to get to know the older girl campers when one requested our help to remove a wasp nest in one of their cabins. We were in the maintenance shed when the call came in and Carl and Bob were immediately off to the rescue. Phil suggested I go too as he knew how the boy/girl dynamics worked at camp. For some reason, I grabbed a can of wasp spray on my way out. Seemed like a good idea.

Once I got to the cabin in question, both Carl and Bob were chatting up the girls, who were all outside on the porch. As far as I could see, nothing had been done about the wasps. If I had been a little worldlier, I might have concluded that the wasps were just a ruse to get the boys to the cabin. I wasn't, so I innocently asked one of the girls who was off to the side where the wasps were. They actually existed and she described the general location in the cabin.

I walked in like a great white hunter, sprayed the nest, and that was that. One of the girls noted that I was the only one who cared to solve their problem, and I felt good about that. I was beginning to see the opportunities and noted that there were a number of good looking girls in the group. I also realized I had stiff competition in Carl and Bob.

The senior campers were staying for two weeks, so there was a dance on the middle Saturday night. Pastor Carl, who was the camp director, played the drums and was the band leader. He had a terrific handlebar mustache and looked the part. He was also a very progressive guy for the era and a perfect camp director. Everybody loved him, his wife, and five little kids. Quite a family.

The staff was invited to the dance, so we all put on clean clothes and Carl, Bob, and I went to check out the chicks. Carl and Bob were both good looking and outspoken, so they quickly identified the girls they were most interested in. To me this was very useful information as I didn't want conflict and I didn't want to be in second place if two of us were interested in the same girl. The good news was that their interests didn't seem to conflict with mine.

I wasn't comfortable asking a girl to dance. Mostly because I feared rejection, but also because my dancing talents were limited. I did however realize from Carl and Bob that the staff guys were considered a catch by the campers. We were clearly fishing out of a barrel. But keep in mind that even if you made a connection, there wasn't much opportunity to do something about it given the normal separation between campers and staff. Nevertheless, the age-old need to make a connection and have someone attracted to you was strong, even at 16.

I guess for me it was an enchanted evening, because across a crowded room I saw a stranger, Alayne Yock, and I was smitten. As I remember I danced with several girls, but mostly with Alayne. At the end of the dance the girls walked back to their cabins and we tagged along. Somewhere along a dark stretch of trail heading to the cabins, we kissed. I was done for, and floated back to the lodge. Carl and Bob also had success, but I could have cared less. To say I was glad I took the job at Camp Biesler would be an understatement.

The rest of the second week I tried to be around the senior campers, with limited success. The time I did have with Alayne just reinforced my decision. Carl and especially Bob were always looking to "trade up" and in the end made no meaningful connections and pissed off more than a few of the girls. I suspect that was more typical, and normal, than my experience, but I was happy.

Alayne's mother picked her up at the end of camp, and Phil and I were introduced. I tripped over myself trying to help load the car with Alayne's stuff, just to be around. She left with the promise to write. No texting in those days. I remember the address all these years later: 153 Ross Avenue. As they drove away, Phil turned to me and said that Alayne's mother was a knockout. I hadn't noticed since Mrs. Yock was an older woman in her 30s, but Phil had a keen appreciation of beauty and he was right. In his mind this seemed to confirm my good judgement and taste. By this time Phil and I had become great friends, but he was still the boss.

Alayne lived in Hackensack and I lived in Cresskill, worlds apart in the 1960s without a car. But I didn't want this summer romance to end, so I decided to write a letter. Without a dictionary and with my limited spelling skills, this was a gigantic challenge. You didn't have spell check or the delete key, so what you wrote was final. A mistake required a cross-out (ugly) or you had to start over with a new piece of paper. I had to think ahead about what I was going to say so I could avoid words I couldn't spell. Since that was most words, the letters must have read like 3rd-grade material. The biggest problem was not knowing what you didn't know. One time I wanted to call Alayne an angel and spelled it angle. I'm sure she overlooked most of my spelling lapses, but not this one. After I got over the embarrassment, which wasn't easy, we laughed about it many times.

During August, Alayne was far away and most of the counselors were girls. It wasn't hard to take a shine to one, especially if there was a little encouragement. This happened a few times with one of the counselors who was several years older than me. I thought this was pretty hot stuff. We spent some time in her cabin on Saturday nights when the camps were changing. Also in a nearby hay field after dark. A lot of heavy petting, but we kept most of our clothes on. One time I was leaving her cabin trying not to have anyone notice. I figured I had a good excuse, being the maintenance guy. After all, light bulbs burned out and had to be changed. Unfortunately, my belt buckle was on the side, hair was flying (I had hair then), and my T-shirt was a bit crinkled. I was fooling no one, as noted by the acid comment from another passing counselor.

The campers left on Saturday noon so if there were no two-week campers around, the afternoon was quiet. We would be working somewhere, often in the woods, and Walter or Pastor Carl would play gospel music over the loudspeakers, sung by Tennessee Ernie Ford. They were great gospel songs and it was like God singing, with Ford's deep voice. If your faith was wavering, one or two songs would restore it.

The other great fun was a trip to the dairy bar in Hackettstown for an ice cream Sunday. Few on the staff had cars, but every so often two or three cars that were available would fill up and head for an after dark treat. It was like breaking out of jail for a few hours, and Phil and Ellen would often come along.

One weekend, when we had a little free time, Bob asked if I wanted to shoot some baskets. He was taller than me and fancied himself a pretty good basketball player. He apparently was on his high school team and thought I would be an easy mark. The way he talked you thought he was the next (white) Bill Russell. He wasn't so hot and I eat his lunch in our first one-on-one game. He found some excuse to stop playing and never asked me to play again. I walked away smiling.

Needless to say, that first summer at Camp was wonderful in all respects. I learned a lot about life from Phil and my confidence was boosted big time with a successful relationship with Alayne. I came back to Cresskill for my senior year a different, and I think better, person.

Next to my parents, Phil became a huge influence on me. He never finished high school, married Ellen, and joined the Army. He spent time in Germany and was a terrific mechanic. He was also functionally illiterate. If you can believe this, he relied on me when it came to spelling, which fortunately wasn't often. His son, Steven, was badly dyslexic, which was diagnosed when he got older. I suspect Phil was too. One day we drove into town to get something at the hardware store and Phil had to write a personal check. He asked me to fill it out, short of his signature, and that's when I realized how difficult spelling and reading were for him.

Nonetheless, he could fix anything. When there was a mechanical problem on one of the camp trucks/cars or any engine anywhere, I was clueless about how to fix it. I expressed my frustration to Phil that I didn't know where to start. He said he didn't either, so he just tried different things and slowly by trial and error, or process of elimination, focused on the problem. Water pump, starter, spark plugs etc., he always found the problem (the hard part) and then he fixed it (the easy part).

I learned quite a bit about cars, which in the 1960s were much simpler than today. No computers, all wrenches and sweat. The best part of the Biesler fleet was the WWII Jeep we used to get around the campgrounds. It was your classic Jeep with a stick shift and a front window that could be turned down. I learned to drive on that Jeep and because of it, I passed my driver's test at the end of the summer with flying colors.

It also had 4-wheel drive, so we took it everywhere off road to collect wood for the campfires. Some weekends there were 4 campfires: 2 groups of campers leaving and 2 groups coming in. The campfires were huge, a cube about 4 feet in each dimension with the larger logs (8 to 10 inches in diameter) on the bottom and a teepee of small kindling on the top. We wanted Pastor Carl to be able to light the fire with one match, which meant carefully constructing the teepee and using dry, dead wood for the rest. We were mostly successful, but it took all day and then some to find, cut, and build four fires.

The best part of the "fleet" was the Jeep and the best part of the Jeep was driving in the hay fields. This had two parts. Before the hay was cut, we would drive through the fields with zero visibility, given that the hay was about 5 to 6 feet high. The thrill of driving fast bordered on the scary, at least for me. Didn't do that too often. After the hay was cut, we would cross the field and stop somewhere. Then we would rev the engine and pop the clutch. The tires would squeal and off we would go, just to stop and do it again. Boys will be boys.

Most of the summer included day after day of routine mainte-nance work: the campfires as mentioned, more painting, keeping the vehicles running, cutting grass, fixing light bulbs, cleaning the heads, and occasionally retrieving a lost ring down the drain. I was good at that, which preceded my lifelong professional work in the wastewater field.

I think the most fun I had was cleaning the brook that fed the pond used for swimming. It was a beautiful brook with riffles and pools that wandered through the woods. It had been dammed to make a small pond with a sandy beach for the campers. Over the years the brook had been clogged with fallen trees, brush, and leaves. For two days, Phil, Bob, and I started from the headwaters and worked our way downstream to the pond, cleaning out the brook. We walked right in the middle of the stream and essentially removed dozens of small debris dams. Every time we would breach a dam there would be a small tsunami headed downstream. The bigger dams were obviously the most fun as the water rushed downstream. This was great field work in hydraulics. Sub critical and super critical flow and all that. Or maybe it was just fun mucking around in the brook and calling it work.

We had one great adventure away from camp. Some good Lutheran had donated a maintenance building to the camp. We really needed one since we kept all the tools and supplies in a small falling down building about the size of a one car garage. It was an overcrowded mess and we spent too much of the day looking for the tools we needed. The new building was huge by comparison, about the width of a three-car garage and over 100 feet long. Unfortunately, it came in pieces and had to be put together. The pieces were corrugated metal over a steel frame.

The first problem was getting all the pieces from the donator's farm to camp, a distance of about 20 miles. Phil got another good Lutheran to donate his coal truck for the transport operation. This had a huge open rectangular trailer where we were going to load the building pieces. Sounds simple.

We got an early 5:30 am start and drove the 20 miles to the farm. The plan was to get everything back to camp in one day, so we all went, Phil, Carl, Bob, and me. It took us all morning to load the truck and it was backbreaking work. The problem was that certain sections were very large and stuck up much higher than the cab on the truck. We weren't too concerned at first until we started to leave the farm and realized that they would be too high to make it under many electric lines and bridges.

Phil stopped at the first offending electric line to consider a plan of attack. The electric lines were easy. While Phil drove slowly, we would take 2x4s and lift the sagging lines over the pieces of sheet metal as we walked from the front to the back of the trailer. We were crazy, but Phil wanted the building badly and we were out in the country without too many cops. Besides we had God on our side.

The bridges weren't so easy, so Phil, from memory and some trial and error, charted a route to avoid bridge underpasses. It took us over six hours to get back to camp, but we made it as light faded. I don't think we had anything to eat, just went right to bed. Our arms were rubber after lifting up a hundred electric lines and walking them over the metal walls while Phil slowly drove forward, stopping when we screamed.

We were stopped by one cop, and Phil played the God card, and for some reason he let us continue with the craziness.

The next morning, with sore muscles all around, we had to unload the truck. After the excitement of the day before, this was just hard work. Now the erector set pieces had to be put together. However, as we all know, a building is only as good as its foundation. This was only a light metal building, but Phil insisted on a foundation for a skyscraper. Concrete footings below the frost line and cinder blocks to grade.

Fortunately, we had a backhoe dig the foundation trench about 3 to 4 feet deep. Then came the concrete trucks to pour the footings. This is when the problems started. We didn't get the footings to dry perfectly level, in fact they weren't level at all, despite our best efforts.

Not to worry, said Phil, we will make up the difference with the cinder blocks.

None of us were very good masons and it was backbreaking work: carrying the cinder blocks to where they were needed, mixing the mortar, and placing the blocks. As I remember, there were four courses of blocks and the goal was to finish with the top course level. 2x10s were then to be placed on top of the cinder blocks and the metal walls were to be secured to the 2x10s.

Since the concrete footings weren't level to begin with, we had to make up the difference with the cinder blocks. Needless to say, this was a disaster, and likely took us three times longer as we screwed around placing each block with no plan or system to make things come out level. When we were done, we still needed to adjust the 2x10s. You see, if the foundation wasn't level, by the time you got to the roof a small discrepancy at the bottom would become a big deal at the top.

The metal pieces were bolted together and the holes had to line up, so a small off-set at the bottom could be tolerated, but as you got higher the bolt holes would get progressively out of alignment and there was no real alternative but to start over. The nightmare was to get 90% done and find out that the small discrepancy at the beginning now prevented you from finishing.

We wanted to move fast, but Phil understood that if we didn't start correctly, we would be building the thing twice. Well, we got it built and we all felt terrific. It was our Taj Mahal, but with a dirt floor and no water. The cost of pouring a concrete floor and running a water line were not in the budget and this would later cause Phil some distress. But for the moment we moved all the vehicles and equipment inside and had space to spare. We were in heaven.

One day shortly after completion, I was walking toward the maintenance building as Phil was coming out. He looked particularly distressed, and I said "what's up?" He mumbled "Oh shit, I sneezed," and held up his false teeth. When he was in the Army, he had all his teeth replaced, and they had popped out when he sneezed. He pointed in the direction of the mess hall, and water, where he was headed to clean them off. Talking without teeth isn't easy, but funny as hell. I laughed so hard my side hurt as Phil hurried up the hill swearing all the way and hoping not to run into anyone else.

One more thing about Phil and Ellen. They loved people and were great ambassadors for the camp, by just being themselves. They weren't hard core Lutherans, just good people and everyone loved them. They had the good fortune to live in the caretaker's house, which was a big old stone building that was a bit run down but had great "bones." The best part was a huge living room with a massive fireplace on one end and the card table at the other. Many an evening the lodge staff would hang around in the living room and a few of us would play pinochle. These games were intense and great fun. It's where I got especially fond of Phil and Ellen and adopted them as extended family, or they adopted me. They were the very best.

So as I was leaving camp for my senior year, I promised Phil I would visit during the winter and come back the next summer. I couldn't think of a better way to spend the next summer, and I think Phil agreed.

11.

BACK FOR SENIOR YEAR

I HAVE ALREADY TALKED at length about high school academics and sports. By all accounts, I was heading into my senior year in a very good place. I had the normal insecurities but felt good about where I was in relationship to sports and class work. Clearly the big issue was how I was going to get into a decent college. The social scene was another thing altogether and my skin problems continued to be a big issue for me.

I was seeing Alayne, but without a car, things were not good. I couldn't drive alone until January when I got my full license. One Saturday I drove to Hackensack with Dad to pick up Alayne for an early September dance at the high school. Once there, we got bored, so walked outside into the warm night and started making out on a small bridge. We lost track of time and Dad got pissed because he couldn't find us to make the trip back to Hackensack. Not the chattiest ride I ever had.

Later in the fall was the time to take the SATs for college admissions. Mom and Dad wanted me to go to college, as Leslie did, and there was never any question about not going. Both Mom and Dad should have gone to college, but it wasn't in the cards in their day. The SATs were on a Saturday and that Friday night Dad made some general comment about getting a good night's sleep. I went out and stayed out a bit too long. He was furious when I strolled in, saying something about jeopardizing my future. He was right of course, but I'm not sure staying out had anything to do with my results. They were just OK, but considering how far I had come, I wasn't too disappointed.

I applied to three schools: Lafayette, University of Pittsburgh, and George Washington University in DC. They all had engineering programs, which the guidance counselors suggested was best for me, for what reason I'm not exactly sure. I only visited Lafayette. Dad and I drove up one day and had an interview. I didn't know much about any of the schools and they all were a stretch. I never had a "safe school" and I'm not sure why.

Our whole class was in an unusual position since the school had no track record. We were the first graduating class. I think this worked in my favor, because I had some terrific recommendations and, if truth be told, I think they carried the day. My academic record wasn't so great, although it showed constant improvement, and sports were good but not world class. I got accepted at Lafayette, and by the time the notice came, it had become my first choice. That's perhaps because Leslie had some experience there and it was her first choice. Honestly, I can't remember if I got into the other two or not. Doesn't matter at this point, but I can't imagine a better experience at another college.

Phil Goshow, my freshman roommate and good friend, always speculated that we were the last two guys accepted in our class given our less than stellar high school academic records and the fact that we were assigned a basement room in South College. Actually, we roomed together only one semester. Our room was so small, they converted it to storage at Christmas. We moved, separately, into slightly better digs vacated by guys who dropped out, but we remained in the basement!

Christmas my senior year in high school was the best, likely because, as I look back, it was the last one with Dad. It was good for other reasons too. First, I could drive alone. There is one universal feeling kids get when they can drive...FREEDOM. In any event, on Christmas Eve I picked up Alayne in the afternoon and came back home for dinner and church. Leslie and Henry were there, and Fred Rehnquist came to join us. He was an American Field Service exchange student from Sweden living with Rich Kletter's family. He was a great guy and was immediately "one of the guys." He was Christian and the Kletters were Jewish, so Mom wisely asked him to join us. It was all quite special.

Sometime around this time I had seen the movie, An Affair to Remember, with Cary Grant and Deborah Kerr. They meet and fall in love on a ship crossing the Atlantic from England to NYC. At the NYC pier they agree to meet at the top of the Empire State Building in a year if they still have feelings for each other. A year later on the way to meet, the Deborah Kerr character is hit by a car, leaving Cary with a broken heart on the 89th floor, thinking he was stood up. Things work out for them, but I was taken by the planned meeting at the Empire State. So, I arranged a trip to NYC with Alayne one night and suggested we visit the observatory at the Empire State. It was quite beautiful and I gave Alayne my high school ring, so we were "pinned." A big commitment for me. It seemed important and quite poignant at the time, but the impact faded rather quickly, complicated by my wandering.

During the basketball season, Rich Kletter, Richie Ewald, and I hung around all the time. There were several girls that rounded out our social group. Carol Fine, who kept both Rich and Richie constantly guessing who was the favored one, and Lynn Mondshein, who I took a shine to. I believe in hindsight we all had good taste. We were a few years ahead of Broadway Joe Namath, in that we didn't believe you needed to be a Spartan to be a good ball player. Enjoying the companionship of lovely young ladies was not to be denied in the pursuit of victory on the field. Hot blood enhanced both experiences.

One night before a game at the end of the basketball season, we found ourselves at Lynn's because her parents weren't home. The couches got a good workout that evening, and fortunately, although I didn't think so at the time, we all kept our clothes on. This however was a big deal because I was still seeing Alayne, although Hackensack seemed a thousand miles away while on the couch.

This created a dilemma that played out over the rest of the school year. Alayne could detect something was wrong and was at a huge disadvantage because of distance. Things came to something of a head at the Hackensack baseball game previously mentioned. Both were in the stands and if words weren't exchanged, looks certainly were. Shortly after, I took a trip to Ross Avenue and told Alayne I was breaking off the relationship. The senior prom was coming up and a decision needed to be made. I always thought I was a good guy to do it face to face, but it's not good causing pain no matter how it happens, and no matter the reasons, it diminishes you.

So Lynn and I went to the senior prom, which I have no memory of. It wasn't because of Lynn, she looked lovely, as the picture shows. After the acceptance at Lafayette and the prom, it was all fun and games until graduation. I started seeing Alayne again, while still seeing Lynn, and it took all my meager talents to keep things straight. Mom understood what I was doing and although didn't encourage it, was decidedly unbothered. This surprised me, but I attribute it in part to the pain she knew was coming with Dad's cancer and that she wanted me to have a carefree time in the waning days of school.

The following illustrates the problems with such an arrangement. But first I'll say from this distance, it's a play that never turns out well. That's because the first casualty is truth and the next casualties are people.

In early June, I was building a patio off the back of the house. I had cleared and graded the space and put in the concrete forms. The concrete truck came one afternoon, pulled into the backyard, and backed up to the patio space and dumped the concrete into the forms. The patio was about 30 feet along the back of the house, extended out about 20 feet. A lot of concrete. I leveled it as best I could, but it was too soupy and needed to firm up a bit to properly smooth out and finish.

At this point, late afternoon, Mom was going to visit Dad in the hospital. She went most every afternoon and I went as often as possible. She knew how bad things were and gently tried to get me to go more often, without telling me the unpleasant details. I assumed I'd see Dad plenty when he got home.

By the time we got back from the hospital, it was getting dark and the concrete was setting too fast for me to finish it the way I wanted. Just the opposite problem from when I left. It was dark and I was getting frustrated. So, I drove the car on the back lawn taking essentially the same route as the 30-ton concrete truck. My plan was to turn the headlights on the patio and continue to work. The 30-ton concrete truck had missed the manhole for the septic tank, but I didn't. One back wheel fell into the tank and it took me some time to jack up the car, put some boards under the wheel, and carefully lower the car and drive it free.

Once done I realized it was too late to make the planned 45-minute drive to Hackensack and see Alayne. Of course, I called her and explained I drove the car into the septic tank. "Sure you did," I heard her say. She wanted to say, "was it your tank or Lynn's?" but she didn't have to. Although it was a true story, who would believe me under the circumstances. The worst part was I actually considered calling Lynn after I hung up with Alayne because driving to her house only took five minutes and the night was still young. Maybe I did, I can't remember.

Graduation, as mentioned, was a blur with Dad in the hospital. Further, I was ready to move on and although I had a pretty good run in high school, I knew in my bones that the best was yet to come. Still feel that about the future.

12.

CAMP BEISLER, 1965

I WENT TO CAMP Beisler one week before graduation to help open the camp as in the previous summer. The good news was Alayne was the assistant Arts and Crafts director and we both were to live in the lodge. Now the tables were switched, and she had the advantage of proximity over Lynn. However, truth be told, if she had lived in Cresskill there never would have been the Lynn diversion.

I was the old hand at camp and life was good. I went back for graduation for two days, but without Dad things were a bit glum. My mind had finished with all things Cresskill and I was on to new things.

During the first few days back, I was beginning to wrap my mind around the fact that Alayne and I were living so close together. Then one day less than a week after I got back, we were working on cleaning up the debris from an old building we had knocked down when Phil got called away. A bit later he came back and said that Pastor Carl wanted to see me because Dad had taken a turn for the worst. Pastor Carl confirmed this and said Mom wanted me to come home. He further said that by chance he was heading in that direction and would drive me home. If true or not, Pastor Carl was the best of the best.

It was a long drive home given that he was the boss and a pastor. I wasn't much good at making small talk, or any talk for that matter. As I was directing him home and he realized we were right around the corner, he told me that Dad had died. I didn't say anything, I couldn't. I motioned where to turn into our driveway, got out, walked up the front steps and into Mom's arms. We hugged as we made it into their bedroom right inside the front door. I sat down and cried my eyes out. Mom tried to explain that she wanted to tell me of Dad's condition but didn't want to ruin my last days of school. Then Dad went so fast before she could warn me.

Mom felt badly, but I understood and in hindsight, it was for the best. I wanted to remember Dad before the illness. I didn't want to remember that weak handshake as he wasted away. He was my hero, and I was proud to be his son.

Funeral arrangements were made and things played out over the next few days. I was in a fog and just went along. As I mentioned, Dad grew up Catholic, but wanted to be cremated. He always said it was a shame that the best real estate in most towns were taken up by the cemeteries.

At the wake and funeral there were men from Con Ed whom I didn't know, but who came up and said my Dad was a good guy. That was a big deal for me. There also were a lot of local people who came, and many were my mother's friends to give her comfort. My friends came too, although at that age it was awkward for us and few words were spoken. As it happened Alayne and Lynn both arrived at the same time, and after paying respects had some time outside to compare notes. This might have been a disaster, but they respected my sorrow and apparently found it most interesting to exchange their stories. At this point it was pretty clear, at least to me, that I had a much deeper interest in Alayne.

The fact is my deepest interest was in Me. I had a serious lack of self-confidence in many areas (e.g., was I going to make it in an engineering program at Lafayette), but on another level, I acted as though my shit didn't stink. I was Master of the Universe; I was entitled to have two girlfriends. Why not when you are filled with the tonic of youth and no one to call you out. Dad always played that role to great effect, but he was gone and I was the man of the house... he had said so.

After the funeral, I went back to camp and Mom went to stay a spell with Aunt Ruth, her oldest and dearest friend. She actually had many friends to spend time with and this helped a great deal. Leslie and Henry went back to Syracuse, where Henry was getting his Ph.D. Both Leslie and I were grateful that Mom had many people to support her, since both of us were now away.

When I got back to camp, I felt awkward as the kid whose father died. But everyone was terrific, especially Phil. He said a quiet "I'm sorry" and then we went to work. The best medicine, at least for me. For the better part of the last 50 years, it has been too hard to talk about Dad, especially with people close to me, but I think of him so very often and wish I had known him better and longer.

Now that I was back at camp, Cresskill faded quickly into the rearview mirror and I started thinking about college, with some trepidation. After all, what did I know about engineering? The only sure thing was my interest in civil engineering, as opposed to other types. That aside, and as usual, I expected to be the dumbest guy in the class. I could have been a wreck thinking about my academic limitations all summer, but fortunately, I had other things to distract me.

First was hard work, which, as mentioned, was the best way for me to avoid feeling sorry for myself. I also had Phil and Ellen to lean on and they made me feel safe and comfortable all summer. This would likely have been enough to make for a wonderful experience in the shadow of my dad's death. What pushed it over the top in a good way, was Alayne's presence on the staff.

After all, we were both living in the lodge, literally within feet of each other. Sure, there was a boy's side and a girl's side to the second floor bedrooms, but there were no grownups in the building. You might think that because this was a church camp everyone was above reproach. Try to tell that to teenagers with raging hormones.

We didn't see each other much during the day and didn't eat at the same table in the mess hall, but in the evening all the staff, including counselors, hung around the first floor of the lodge or played cards next door in Phil and Ellen's living room.

I felt very much at home in this atmosphere. I knew my way around and was accepted almost as an equal by Phil. However, those raging hormones and incredible access was bound to cause some issues.

I'm not sure how things got started, it really doesn't matter, but after a week or so of sleeping in the rooms, someone suggested we sleep on the back porch. This was presumably to benefit from the cool country night air. The porch was off the second level and ran the full length of the back of the building. There were doors to the porch from both sides of the second floor.

As luck would have it, the porch was just wide enough to accommodate the mattresses with a narrow lane along the outside railing to access your location. The length of the porch could have accommodated 10 to 12 mattresses side to side. Not everyone slept outside, likely five or six of us. Several guys and several gals.

One funny incident before we move to the porch activities. Walter Blue, the assistant camp director, slept on the boys' side of the lodge with the rest of us. That included the kitchen and maintenance staff and Ralph Zobis, who was my roommate and the waterfront director. Ralph was a few years older than me and Walter was six years older. Walter had been at the camp for some time, overlapping with Leslie. As noted, he had dated Leslie, so I had known him for some time. The dating part had long since ended by the time I arrived at camp.

During the dating period, Walter came to Cresskill with Leslie for a weekend. Walter went to Muhlenberg College right across the brook from Cedar Crest. I think they met at camp, and just happened to go to adjacent colleges. I also can't remember if they came to Cresskill from camp or college, but it doesn't matter. Things went well on Saturday at least as far as I knew, but for some reason, Walter was a no-show at breakfast Sunday morning. He had gotten up during the middle of the night and left. So I guess things hadn't gone so well on Saturday. Walter was an odd ball, which was fun for everyone, except his girlfriends. Walter's bail-out in the middle of the night became family legend and generated much laughter in its many re-tellings. Henry, Leslie's husband of more than 50 years, was also, by some measures, a bit odd, but in a far better way than Walter. Leslie did well to wait for "The Henry." More on Henry later.

Walter was a French major, very artistic, very smart, and danced to his own drummer. Like many others with his talents, he was great company, but hard to live with. It was also well-known around the lodge that nothing woke up Walter in the middle of the night. So we concocted a plan to lift him up in his bunk in the wee hours and carry him out to the field in back of the lodge. We thought he would have quite an awakening to the morning sun in the great outdoors, perhaps covered with a bit of dew.

There were two difficult parts to this prank. First was to dislodge the top bunk, where Walter slept, from the bottom one. Second was the journey down the back steps from the second floor porch. This was all made more difficult given that Walter was not a little guy, pushing 200 lbs.

Four of us, one at each corner of the bed, did the deed and laughed all the way back to bed. Unfortunately, despite Walter's sound sleeping habit and because of our sloppy execution, he woke in the early stages of the move. Being a great sport, he pretended not to notice and endured the trip down the back steps and into the field. He put up with the good fun and, in a way, was honored that we paid so much attention to him. We all had a good laugh the next day.

Now back to the porch. For the first few nights we each slept in our sleeping bags. It was generally boy/girl/boy/girl, but the only real couple was Alayne and me. We had the last two spaces at the end of the porch, on the opposite side from the back steps. There were two ways to access the porch. One was from the two halls that served the men and women sides of the second floor. These two doors opened side by side in the middle of the porch. The second way was up the back steps, which were open air from the back of the lodge at one end of the porch.

Whether it was intentional or not, Alayne and I were positioned as far away as possible from anyone who might happen on the porch, think Pastor Carl. Now you might also think that this sleeping arrangement might be frowned upon by the powers that be, also think Pastor Carl. It was certainly not a secret. Walter slept in the lodge with us and although he didn't prefer the porch, knew what was going on. So did Pastor Carl. Actually, there was not much that Pastor Carl didn't know.

Nevertheless, nothing was said about the sleeping arrangement. Sort of a nightly co-ed sleep over. Getting in and out of sleeping bags is a pain in the ass. So after a few nights we decided to completely unzip the sleeping bags and use one below and the other as a blanket above. This took away all the appearance of sleeping separately, although we took the sleeping bags into our rooms every day in part to keep them out of bad weather and also to avoid advertising the sleeping arrangement.

I was 17 at the beginning of the summer and Alayne was 16. We were effectively sleeping together every night and as you might expect, one thing led to another. Since it was a bit awkward with our close-by neighbors on the porch, when the hormones were raging we sometimes went into Alayne's room on the women's side and had a bit more privacy. This was a mistake, because it was a clear violation of the rules.

Pastor Carl occasionally call an all staff meeting to keep everyone up to date on camp activities. At one of these meetings he mentioned, without naming names, that it was strictly against camp rules for the men to cross to the women's side of the Lodge and vice versa. He didn't need to name names; everyone knew who he was talking about. I wanted to melt into the woodwork! Needless to say, he got his point across and we stopped the practice. But the co-ed sleepovers continued on the porch. Just amazing! After the meeting, one of the counselors said to me that she knew our motto was "Sin Lutheran," but this was taking it a bit too far. Actually, I think she was jealous because she had to sleep with the campers.

Amy, one of the counselors, was dating Ralph, my actual roommate. They later had a long happy marriage. Her parents also happened to have had a summer cabin in the Pocono Mountains, about two hours from camp. One weekend we were given 24 hours off from Saturday noon to Sunday noon. Amy suggested that the four of us take Ralph's car and go to the cabin.

So off we went, Ralph and Amy in the front seat and Alayne and I in the back. It was a long drive, made longer by a rainstorm in the Poconos. This wouldn't have been so bad, except the windshield wipers were powered off some sort of air compressor. The problem was the air shut down when the car accelerated. So we were fine going downhill, but blind going uphill in the heavy rain. Ralph tried to gain enough speed going downhill, bad enough, so he could wait as long as possible to hit the gas on the next hill. It was scary, and amazing we didn't wind up around a tree.

Once at the cabin our blood pressure dropped, and we had dinner. Amy's parents weren't there so after dinner, in the twilight, we all went skinny dipping in the lake and had a great time. Slept together that night.

As you can imagine, I was sad when the summer ended and I headed off to college, with a different kind of roommate, and Alayne headed back to Hackensack for her senior year. I never talked about my love life with the guys partly because no one would believe my story of summer nights on the porch. Paradise found and lost!

Because of Dad's death in June, Mom requested additional financial aid from Lafayette. I'm not sure what it was originally, but it was increased to a scholarship for the first year and a loan for the second year. This equated to a scholarship of $3,000 and a loan of $3,000 (which I was to pay off at essentially zero interest). Dad's life insurance policy from Con Ed was $10,000, so Mom had the remaining $6,000 available. How times have changed from a college education costing 12 grand.

As part of this change, I had to go to the college to sign some papers. Camp was only about an hour from Lafayette, but I didn't have a car. As luck would have it, one of Alayne's friends from Hackensack, Janie, had been given a new bright blue Ford Mustang convertible. This was the second year for the Mustang line and the car was already a classic.

Janie let me borrow it for the afternoon and off I went with the top down and the sun shining. For a few hours, I was Rick on Route 66, and managed to bring the car back without a scratch.

After the horrible beginning with Dad's death, the summer was a 10 out of 10, but now it was time to see what I was made of at the college level.

Family, 1957

Leslie, Dad and Rick, 1960

FAMILY

Mom and Rick, 1958

Leslie, Henry and Dad, 1964

Dad

Mom

Honeymoon 1944
Niagara Falls

EARLY YEARS

First day of School

Leslie and Rick, 1952

Rick and Trip, 4th of July 1955

8th Grade, Mike on the right. Rick 5th from the right

Rick and Dad, 1958

Maine

Little League

Robin Hood

HIGH SCHOOL

Basketball-Big Win

Cresskill High Wallops Emerson Cagers, 64-19

Cougars Boost Record To 4-1 As Four Hit Double Figures; Cavaliers Drop Seventh

Cresskill — Four players scored in double figures as Cresskill thumped arch-rival Emerson, 64-19, last night. The victory was the Cougars' fourth in five games and third in a row.

It was the seventh defeat for the winless Cavaliers.

HILPERTS NETS 17

Jerry Hilperts led the Cresskill rout with 17 points. Rich Kletter and Rich Ewald hit for 12 apiece while Moore tallied 11.

Kim Mazzola was the only Cougar starter who wasn't in twin figures. He had eight to match Ken Mc Loughlan's output, which was high for Emerson.

Hilperts and Ewald excelled in the first quarter to give Cresskill a 10-3 lead at the quarter. The Cougars built their lead to 29-9 at the intermsion

and coasted home the rest of the way, building their edge as the game progressed.

Cresskill also romped in the junior varsity game, 62-27.

The box score:

Cresskill (64)				Emerson (19)			
	G.	F.	P.		G.	F.	P.
Hilperts	8	1	17	Harms	0	2	2
Kletter	5	2	12	McLoughlin	3	2	8
Lo Cicero	0	0	0	Bing	1	0	2
Ewald	5	2	12	Bush	0	0	0
Moore	5	1	11	Dienstbach	0	0	0
Krulik	0	0	0	Kesper	2	0	4
Mazzola	4	0	8	Mannes	1	0	2
Mc Connell	0	0	0	Doughty	0	0	0
O'Rourke	2	0	4				
Scott	0	0	0				
Totals	29	6	64	Totals	7	5	19

SCORE BY PERIODS

| Cresskill | 10 | 19 | 19 | 16 | — | 64 |
| Emerson | 3 | 6 | 2 | 8 | — | 19 |

Referee — Melsee. Umpire — Clancey.

Leslie's Wedding, Rick and Dad

Camp, Rick and Alayne

Football, Kim and Rick

Senior Prom,
Rick and Lynn

COLLEGE

Rick and Alayne, 1968

1969

Rick and Alayne, 1969

SPORTS

Babe Ruth All Star Team, 1961

High School Football, Rick kicking the extra point

Basketball Team, 1931, Dad, top row on the right

IF weekiend 1968

Chi Phi Roll

EDWARD AHART Philipsburg, N J
WILLIAM BATES Schenectady, N Y
JOHN BAUMANN Westfield, N J
JEROME BLAKESLEE Broadheadsville, Pa.
C. PETER BLOUIN III Augusta, Me.
STEPHAN BOALS West Chester, Pa.
THOMAS BRADSHAW Springfield, Mass.
ALLAN BRAGGIN Riverdale, N J
RALPH BRAINARD Scotch Plains, N J
WILLIAM BRECHT Bryn Mawr, Pa.
JOHN CAREY Kingston, Pa.
WARREN COLE West Hartford, Conn.
RICHARD CONTEL Hanover Pa.
JAMES DAVIDSON Washington, D. C.
REYNOLD DREWS Larchmont, N Y
TIMOTHY ELY Pelham, N Y
STEPHAN EVANS Wyomissing, Pa.
RAYMOND EWING Oakhurst, Pa.
BRIAN FARLEIGH Easton, Pa.
ROBERT FASOLI Hawthorne, N J
JAMES FLANNERY Shenandoah, Pa.
CARL FREEMAN Edgewood Arsenal, Md.
PETER HALSTEAD Stamford, Conn.
ROBERT HAMILL Portland, Pa.
FREDERICK HARPER Lafayette Hill, Pa.
DENNIS HENDERSON Bridgetown, N J
JAMES HENNESSEY New Providence, N J
WILLIAM HEWLETT Smoke Rise, N J

GARY HILKERT Ramsey, N J
WALTON HILL Upper Darby, Pa.
ROGER HONTZ Hatboro, Pa.
GEORGE IMEL Saylorsville, Pa.
BRUCE JAGGARD Stroudsburg, Pa.
JOHN KEHOE Pittsburgh, Pa.
PETER KENNEDY Sea Girt, N J
THOMAS LA CONTE Wayne, N J
MICHEAL LUBIN Oceanside, N Y
KEITH MALCOLM Garden City, N J
FESTUS McCUE Eastchester, N Y
RICHARD MOORE Cresskill, N. J.
PHILIP MOSEMAN Kingston, Pa.
JEFFREY NEBEL Union, N J
JAMES NELSON Mt. Lakes, N J
R. THOMAS OKONAK Latrobe, Pa.
DONALD PROUGH Allentown, Pa.
ROBERT RANDALL Garden City, N Y
ORVILLE REICH Valley Steam, N Y
RICHARD ROSEN Scarsdale, N. Y
RICHARD SHRINER Weston, Mass.
JON SCHWARTZ Meadowbrook, Pa.
EMIL O. SOMMER III Armonk, N Y
GORDON WETMORE Mendham, N J
GREGORY WILCOX Warwick, R. I.
FILIP YESKEL Hillside, N J
GREGORY YOUNG Schuykill Haven, Pa.

13.

LAFAYETTE COLLEGE, FRESHMAN YEAR

AS I MENTIONED, WHEN Mom and I arrived the first day at Lafayette, we found my room was in the basement of South College. South College was one of the first buildings built on campus and had taken a beating over the years. The college was founded in 1826, so the building was old, but fortunately it had been well-built. My roommate was Phil Goshow and that was a bit of good luck. We got along fine and I loved his record collection, especially the Platters. During the semester, if I got a bit down, I would play the Platter's 33rpm LP. Great songs to this day. My favorite was "The Great Pretender."

Our room was small, but we made out fine. Between classes, meals, and the library, we didn't spend much time there. Sleeping late also helped. Although we didn't say it directly, we both were petrified that we would flunk out as the dumbest guys in the class. Oh yes, it was all guys at Lafayette at the time.

All engineers took the same classes the first two years and then selected a major. Your choices were: civil, chemical, electrical, mechanical, metallurgical, or industrial. Even as freshman, most had a preference, as I did with civil. Your first semester courses were calculus, chemistry, statics (mechanics), English, and one elective, in my case economics. Except for the elective, these subjects were continued, as part two, in the second semester. Statics I and II were actually part of a series that continued into sophomore year with two more classes: Strength of Materials and Dynamics.

Charlie Best, one of our professors, wrote a textbook on Statics, so, as no surprise, we used it. I was intimidated enough but having the author of the textbook teaching the class was scary. It felt like if you didn't do well, not only would your grade point average suffer, but you would be insulting the author/professor. In a backhanded way, you would be saying that both his lectures AND his book were too confusing, and you didn't understand. Convoluted thinking for a first semester freshman, but the reality.

Since I was scared, I worked hard and except for some difficulty with calculus, wasn't overwhelmed. That said, I was shooting for gentlemen Cs and for the most part got them, with an occasional B for good measure. In those days, before grade inflation, a C was fine with me, and many others. There weren't that many As. All the professors had been teaching for a long time and had the lectures down to a science. Speaking of science, I hated the chemistry labs. This is partly because they were on Saturday morning from 8 to 11 am. Ugg!

You got three credits for each class except Chemistry, where you got four because of the lab. Most classes were an hour Monday, Wednesday, and Friday, or an hour and half on Tuesdays and Thursdays. Thursday and Saturday at 11 am were set aside for hour exams that everyone took together. On Saturday morning I had a three-hour chemistry lab, often followed by an hour exam. This severely limited Friday night activities and the possibility of going home on weekends, which turned out to be a good thing.

In addition to regular class, you had a choice of either taking gym or ROTC. Incidentally, 1965 was the first year that chapel wasn't required at Lafayette. Thank God, any God. I chose ROTC because I wanted to be commissioned in the Army when I graduated. Technically, ROTC was just an elective your freshman and sophomore years, and you could have opted out any time. Beginning your junior year, you had to commit to the Army and the Army had to officially accept you. No one was ever rejected, as far as I could tell, and once accepted you were "in the Army." So starting your junior year, you got a $50 dollar/ per month stipend. This was reason enough to join, as $50 bucks more than covered your monthly beer money.

Sometime in late October my freshman year I received a notice from my draft board classifying me as 1A and directing me to Fort Dix to be sworn in as a private. This was before the lottery, and subsequently the all-voluntary Army. Needless to say, I was nervous and immediately went to the head of the ROTC contingent, a full bird colonel. I told him my predicament and he seemed to understand until he looked at the grades I had gotten on an Army test given earlier in the semester. Now I'm not good at taking tests but this was ridiculously easy, and I knew I had done well.

The colonel, with a serious look, noted that I was in the engineering program and yet did poorly on the math part of the exam. This guy held my future in his hands, so I didn't want to say he was crazy, but did register some disbelief. He must have thought something was funny, so took another look at his computer printout and realized he was looking at someone else's grade. I passed, actually with a high mark, and my heart went back to its normal rate. He turned sunny and said he would write the draft board to get me re-classified to ROTC status. I think I signed something to commit to four years of ROTC, but at that point I would have signed anything. I was back in college!

Now, things are never as simple as they seem in the Army. Before the colonel would agree to write the letter, he had a small favor to ask. It was a "quid pro quo." It seemed the ROTC rifle team was short of shooters. The price for the letter was to join the rifle team. I would have joined any team, but the only problem was that the team practiced at Easton High School because the college didn't have a rifle range. Getting there two times a week was a pain, but a small price to pay considering. I hated rifle practice and quit as soon as I could, but at least I learned how to shoot. We shot 22s and I was good in the prone, kneeling, and sitting positions; not so good standing up.

With rifle practice added to my schedule I was busy, but still had a bit of the homesickness bug. It's hard to get rid of. To get home, I would hitchhike down Route 22, usually into NYC, and then take a bus home. Not too many people were heading directly to Cresskill. A few times Mom came to visit, which was always good for a meal out, but heightened the homesickness when she left. One or two times she brought Alayne and we tried to get some private time to rekindle the summer bliss. It wasn't the same.

Lafayette's policy was for the whole freshman class to bond the first semester, so fraternities were off limits. Consequently, the first semester was boring socially, but likely was the main reason I didn't flunk out. Even on weekends there wasn't much to do except study. I also decided not to play football and that was a good decision. It would have taken a huge amount of time and might have sunk my grades, to say nothing of my limited abilities. Sure, I was a high school standout, but would have been mediocre at best in college football.

Actually, many of the best players were engineers and became ineligible to play when mid-semester grades came out. I would have made the cut, as you needed to maintain a 2.0 (C) average, but didn't regret the decision one bit.

I had Dr. Richman for freshman English and actually liked the course. It was all about detective stories and mostly we read short ones. For me they weren't really short, but better than Moby Dick. I was still a pathetically slow reader and my spelling on exams was miserable, but I got my gentleman C. Good old Dr. R. had pity on engineers. He was about 5 feet tall and impeccably dressed for every class. This experience made me believe that if you want kids to enjoy reading you should teach them something they can relate to, not 19th Century English or American literature. Everyone is not an English major.

Since Lafayette was all male, the college arranged two Saturday night mixers during the first semester. One with Cedar Crest, a 4-year college in Allentown PA to the west, where Leslie went, and Centenary, a 2-year college in Hackettstown, NJ, to the east. When you inquired about what to expect, you often heard the expression: Cedar Crest for class and Centenary for ass. This was not true, but myths die hard.

The mixers were something to look forward to but were dreadful affairs. The girls got bussed in and entered our converted dining room en masse. Slowly, as the music played, mingling occurred. It always started with "What is your name and where are you from?" At one of the events, after asking one of the lovelies to dance, she popped the question. Like the first day in Miss Pitts' English class, something overcame me and I answered, "James...James Bond." She clearly didn't have a sense of humor and that was that. Never tried it again, but I should have.

Pete Marks was one of my fellow freshman engineers and I knew him casually from classes. One day we were leaving lunch at the same time and stopped to talk about something. For some reason we found out that we had both recently lost our fathers. Maybe because I hardly knew him, but I found I could talk about the loss without going to pieces. We spoke maybe 15 or 20 minutes, the longest I have ever stayed on the subject. It was good, but not enough.

At Thanksgiving, Mom picked me up and we went to Henry's mother's in Lancaster, Pennsylvania Dutch Country. It was like heaven getting away from classes and exams. Peg always treated me nicely, but she was tough on her boys, Henry and his brother Pete. A strong-minded Dutch woman, she was born in a time when strong, talented woman had to stay at home. Her father was apparently just as tough, owned the Posey Iron Works in Lancaster and subscribed to the notion that a woman's place was in the home. Consequently, he prevented Peg from moving up and running the Iron Works, which I think she could have done with one arm tied behind her back.

In any event, because of this or not, she could be difficult with her sons and daughters-in-law. Three things I remember about that Thanksgiving weekend in chronological order. First, on Thanksgiving morning we loaded up shotguns and went to Bucky Buckwilder's farm, one of Pete's friends, for a pheasant hunt. I thought this was the coolest thing in the world, and the farm was huge. This was an annual event and about 25 folks showed up, all men and their sons and me.

We lined up at one end of a field and slowly walked through it with our guns loaded and pointed down range. I think I had a single barrel, breech loaded 20-gauge shot gun. As we flushed a bird and it started to fly, the shooting began. There were so many folks that the poor birds didn't stand a chance. I thought there were plenty of birds for everyone to take a few home for the stew pot. Some of the older men thought otherwise.

To satisfy the blood lust, a number of birds from a caged area were rounded up and let loose in a nearby field. As they were flushed out people couldn't fire fast enough, and the shooting continued until all were dead or forgotten. Even I, who thought the hunt was a great event, couldn't participate in this final carnage. Everything was done by noon and then it was back to Peg's for the Thanksgiving meal.

Dinner had the usual turkey and fixings, but there was one item new to me. Dried corn. Now I'm a big corn lover so I eat more than my share and have associated Thanksgiving dinner with dried corn ever since. Good stuff if prepared correctly, which takes two days.

Third and last was my recollection of the choice of TV programs in the evening. We were sitting in the living room and I must have been looking at the TV guide, having not seen much TV at school in the last several months. I noticed there was a documentary on the life of JFK, who had been shot just three years prior. I thought this would be terrific to see and said so, to complete silence. Then someone changed the subject and after a short time, Mom asked me to get something she needed in her room upstairs. She followed me up and explained that Peg couldn't stand JFK, because he was Catholic. The documentary showed JFK in a positive light and this would have been too much for Peg to bear without causing a scene.

Needless to say we watched something else, but it gave me a glimpse of who Peg was, despite how nice she was to me. So much for Christian values, but unfortunately a situation I experienced again later with my wife Cynthia's parents.

After Thanksgiving it was back to Easton, PA for a week or two of classes and then final exams before we left for Christmas break. Lafayette was ahead of its time by finishing the semester before the break. Most schools had the Christmas vacation and then exams in

January, which made for a fun vacation. Now almost all schools end the semester before Christmas. By doing this, you have a study-free vacation well into January.

Lafayette also had the tradition of coming back a week early in January to pledge a fraternity. This was also a good idea, since you weren't going to class at the same time you were pledging. Pledging of course created another fear, of being left out, especially because of the terrifying blackball system. When the brotherhood was discussing if a particular freshman would be given an invitation to join, any brother could cast a blackball for no stated reason, and the invitation was killed.

Like any courtship, both sides are trying to sell something and are on their best behavior. I went to open houses at several fraternities and tried to sell myself. There was some information in the rumor mill about what each fraternity was about (jocks, prep schools, Jewish etc.), but for some reason I had very limited information. Again, I didn't have high expectations and was hoping to get into a "C" house, just like my grades. I did visit several of the so-called cool houses as well as one or two "safe" houses. There were about 25 fraternities on campus and almost everyone who was interested could be accommodated by one.

There were also two social clubs, which were similar in format to fraternities. They had beautiful buildings that looked similar to the many fraternity houses. Rich Ewald (no more Richie), who also went with me from Cresskill to Lafayette, joined Watson Hall, one of the social clubs. His brother, several years older, was also a member. Rich was a hippie before it was cool to be one and had a real problem with the exclusionary philosophy of fraternities. He was right in part, but the reality in the mid-'60s was that fraternities ruled at Lafayette. As we shall see, the problems were small, even then, and were far outweighed by the benefits.

One more note about Rich. We were close in high school but hung around with different folks in college. He wanted to go to Princeton or Yale, but didn't get in. Unlike me, Rich was smart, and Lafayette was his safe school. It further irritated him that his uncle was Dean of Students. He started Lafayette with a bit of a chip on his shoulder. I, on the other hand, was thrilled to have been accepted.

Pledging was a big event, since you were going to be associated with the fraternity for the next 3 and a half years. I didn't quite appreciate this at the time, but I got lucky. I liked Chi Phi and they had a terrific house, the physical plant. The brotherhood was supposedly on the upswing and had a strong class just ahead of us. I received an invitation and accepted. Phil got into Phi Gamma Delta (Fiji), which was one of the first-tier fraternities, also in a beautiful house. We had talked about pledging together, which was common among freshmen friends, but it didn't happen. We were both happy about where we ended up, but strangely didn't know much about the rest of our pledge classes.

Here again, I lucked out and slowly found out what a good group of guys I had joined. The upper classmen were also a good group. Very few seniors, more juniors, and a strong sophomore class. A total of about 70 brothers, with about 20 in our pledge class.

As mentioned, the house, called Vallamont, was built as a fraternity in 1908 and was owned by the Rho Chapter of Chi Phi. The national fraternity had 30 to 40 chapters around the country, mostly in the south where it got started. The northern liberals speculated that the "blackball" originated in the conservative south and as the name implies, was intended to keep Black folks OUT. This was not accurate, but made sense given the times. The interesting thing was that Lafayette was almost all white, as was our pledge class. During pledge week, the few Black guys, and they weren't all football players, were actually in high demand. There just weren't enough of them to go around. No one talked about this, but it should have been no surprise that most of the fraternities were all white. By the way, in my last three years I don't remember one time when a blackball was used in secret. Guys were turned down of course, but it was during open discussion.

The house had 26 beds. The rest of the brotherhood lived in dorms. There were off-campus apartments, but few lived off campus. The house had a basement, four upper floors, and a terrific wrap-around porch. It looked like a huge southern mansion, far too nice for college kids. The house faced a large lawn surrounded by other buildings. On one side was another fraternity, DTD, which looked similar to Vallamont.

On the other side, separated by a driveway, was a steep cliff dropping off to beautiful downtown Easton. The driveway looped around the house with parking in the rear. Because of the difference in elevation, the rear door to the parking lot opened from the basement. If you were driving around the house and went off the road, you had a 500-foot fall into Bushkill Creek below. Bushkill Creek entered the Delaware River another half mile downstream.

The basement had two bedrooms (four beds) in rather small spaces, and these were the least attractive in the house. The kitchen, TV room, and Rock Room were also in the basement. More on the Rock Room later. Also in the basement was an apartment of sorts for the cook. Everyone, no matter where they lived, took meals at the house. Meals were served Monday through Saturday lunch. You were on your own Saturday night and Sunday.

The first floor was impressive. It had a huge central foyer. On the left as you entered the foyer was the living room, with a large fireplace, and a billiards room, with a world class table. The living room opened to the side porch that looked over the cliff. Pretty cool. To the right, and in mirror image, was the dining room and a general purpose room that was used to play cards, usually bridge. It also had the only phone in the house, except for one in the president's suite on the second floor. Making a private call on the main phone was impossible.

The main entrance was in the middle of the foyer and opposite the entrance were the stairs to the upper floors. There were six suites on the second floor. Each had a central room with two small attached bedrooms. These were the best and one of them had a phone. That was a big deal in those days, so it was always taken by the president. There was one bathroom with several sinks, showers, and commodes. I don't remember this being a problem, but time blurs one's memory.

The third floor was similar, with smaller rooms and not always two separate bedrooms. The fourth floor was really an attic and had the Chapter Room and some storage. The Chapter Room was where the fraternity rituals were conducted. They included initiations and business meetings. In keeping with tradition, you wore robes, but we didn't take this too seriously. For example, I never learned the secret handshake or mumbo-jumbo phrases to identify yourself to another brother. We took all that to be silly. We were just a group of guys trying to get by and have some fun. The bonding, and it was significant, was forged as a result of shared experiences, not rituals.

The Rock Room was special and well-known campus wide. It was a great attraction during pledging and although I don't remember, it must have made an impression on me. It was not part of the original house, but rather a space under the porch at the end on the house between the main building foundation and the outer porch foundation. It was about 12 feet wide and L-shaped, running all along the cliff side of the house and turning under the front porch for about 20 feet to complete the L. There were openings at each end, knocked through the building foundation walls. The interior walls in the room were bare stone, the ceiling was the porch deck with exposed support beams, and there was no heat.

There was a long wooden table the length of the main leg of the "L" (think Tom Jones feasts without utensils) and the best parts were the decorations and the bar. Empty bottles hung from the ceiling and over the years the brothers had collected (stolen) signs from all over the Lehigh Valley and beyond. The signs were hung throughout. Small street signs and large ones of all sorts. Signs from Intercourse, PA and one huge "Falling Rock" sign. It gave a lot of character to the room and baited the pledge class to get a few new ones.

The bar was at the end of the long leg toward the back of the house and right by the main entrance. There was a tap system and as I remember, we were on tap our whole senior year. Despite 24/7 access to cold beer, the Rock Room was quiet and damp during most of the week. It came alive on Thursday night through the weekend. The main advantage, other than the ambiance, was that you could do almost anything and it could be cleaned up with a hose, without destroying the rest of the house.

I called Mom and told her I had been accepted in a fraternity and was pleased about where I ended up. She had no idea if this was good or bad, but as always was happy for me. Leslie, on the other hand, had an opinion, which she was more than happy to share with me. While at Cedar Crest, she had a blind date with a guy from Chi Phi. One of her friends also had a date and the two guys turned out to be jerks. To get away from their boorishness, the two girls locked themselves in a second floor suite. As the guys were banging on the door, the two climbed out a window onto the roof over the porch, walked around to another window, in another suite, and climbed back in. Shortly thereafter they made their escape back to Cedar Crest.

Keep in mind this was at night and on the end of the house that faced the cliff and Easton below. Perhaps a bit scary. Leslie told the story in great detail, which wasn't a great endorsement of Chi Phi. I took it in stride, told her she and her friend were quite resourceful, and that I would never cause the scene to be replayed.

Second semester was dominated by keeping my grade point average around 2.5. I think I had all Cs and one B first semester, for about a 2.3 GPA. I considered that a success. Second semester, I felt more comfortable and might have gotten 2 Bs. As mentioned, it was more of the same, I still hated chemistry lab and overall I applied myself about the same as first semester.

Like first semester, I considered this a success, especially given the duties associated with a pledge class. We were pledges all second semester and were initiated as brothers at the end of the week before classes started our sophomore year. That week was affectionately called Hell Week. More on that later.

The pledging process, along with blackballs and drinking, are where fraternities get a bad name. Let me explain the process and you can be the judge. The idea of pledging is to develop a bond among your pledge classmates. The first thing done is to assign an upper classman to be your big brother. In my case it was Rich Mellon. He was one guy, as I think of it, who lived off campus in an apartment. He had flunked out, took a year off, and was back. He also was a terrific skier and on the ski patrol at one of the mountains in the Poconos.

Rich was a good guy but was off every weekend skiing and the fraternity wasn't a high priority for him. He offered to take me skiing with a place to bunk with the ski patrol, but I didn't have the money to rent skis, let alone buy a lift ticket even with free lodging. I regret not taking him up on his offer, but that's water under (over) the dam. Consequently, I didn't see Rich much and we never developed a relationship.

As soon as pledge week ended and the incoming class was finalized, the nice guy act ended abruptly. Our first assignment as pledges was to memorize all the brothers' names and hometowns as well as the history of Chi Phi, national and local. The whole idea, other than helping you get to know everyone, was to stage quizzes. Typically, the word would go out in the evening, say 9 pm, that all the pledges were to assemble at the house. We would be lined up in the foyer and the pledge master would yell that we were a bunch of shitheads and fire questions at us. If you didn't get the answer right, it was down for 10 push-ups or a whack on the ass with a paddle.

It was pretty harmless. The most effective part of hazing was not the physical push-ups, but the mental challenge. Mental testing required a bit more originality and was more fun, especially if you were a brother. In short, fear was a much stronger motivator than physical stress. I was hopeless in memorizing the information and worried about it, only to realize after a while that the punishments weren't too bad.

Sometimes we were sent on missions, most frequently to get pizza for a brother late in the evening. We were not allowed to write down the order and were expected to get it right. Fortunately, Rich Mellon didn't live in the House and rarely asked me to do anything. I was thrilled.

Occasionally, when the whole class was punished for some myste-rious infraction, we were told to run the Miracle Mile. Since we were on a hill, we started high, ran down the road that was the back entrance to the college, along Bushkill Creek and back up the hill via a series of steps separated by steep ramps. These steps were brutal and stressed everyone to the limit. Many had to walk the last several hundred steps.

Finishing at the end of the pack meant more push-ups. No one was on the cross-country team.

Of course, when we were lined up in the foyer and elsewhere, certain brothers were worse than others. Those with a bit of a sadistic streak were quickly identified and avoided when possible. This was important because there was a tradition that at some time during the semester the pledges were to kidnap a brother and get some revenge.

There was some discussion, but it was quickly decided that Don Miller was our candidate. He was an electric engineer, a bit of a nerd, and lived on the second floor with a fellow EE and a fish tank. They had wired the lighting in the fish tank to blink with the music that was playing on their stereo. Very cool and the girls loved it. Nor sure about the fish.

They were both smart, but Don had crossed the line a few times in his attempt to tame the pledges. He was therefore a marked man. We conspired to abduct him at night on his way back to the house from the library. Once our lookouts spotted him leaving the library, the plot was initiated. We had Carl Freeman's car in the parking lot behind the house ready to go. Actually Carl was the only one with a car (one of Ralph Nader's Corvairs), so we had no choice.

As Don approach the house, Carl drove to the top of the driveway and waited. Jim Flannery (Shenny), Peter McCue, and I came out from behind parked cars in front of the house, overpowered Don, and stuffed him in Carl's back seat. He knew what was going on from the outset.

With Phase One complete, we moved to Phase Two. Our plan was to drive to the Jersey Shore and threaten to bury him in the sand up to his neck at low tide. Carl was driving and Shenny was shotgun, slowly explaining our plan to Don. Peter and I were in the backseat, with Don in between. Don was about 5'6" and 160 lbs. soaking wet. Peter was 6'3' at 230 lbs. and I was 6'1" at 210 lbs. Don wasn't going anywhere.

Every so often, Shenny would pause and Peter would grunt. Don was beginning to think we were just crazy enough to do as we said. I had to force myself from bursting into laughter, but slowly I too began to believe Shenny.

This was in March so by the time we crossed the bridge to Seaside Heights heading to Long Beach Island, it was about 11pm, and the main drag was dark and deserted. I suspect partly because of the hour, the fact that there were no other cars in sight and Carl's car had Maryland plates, we were pulled over by the local police. It wasn't Carl's erratic driving, they just wanted to check us out. By then Don was in a high level of distress and quickly realized that this was his way out. He said we needed to release him, or he would start screaming. Having no real choice, out he went.

Once the cops determined we were harmless, they let us go with Don standing in the middle of the road explaining his predicament to the cops. We drove away bullshit angry about our bad luck. Now we were on a dead-end street which ended at Long Beach State Park. So after several miles we turned around and headed back toward the bridge, the only way off the barrier island.

We had fucked up and knew we were going to be made a laughing-stock once back at the house. Not much was said. As we approach the bridge, we noticed someone hitchhiking. Upon a closer look, it turned out to be Don. The cops had only driven him to the city limits, the beginning of the bridge. Now Don made a mistake. He ran onto the bridge. I followed and recaptured him mid-bridge.

We were in a rage about his escape and promised to follow through with our original plan. Peter escorted/dragged Don to the water's edge and told him to start digging. There was terror in Don eyes and after a few minutes we all laughed and left him on his knees with the tide coming in.

We got back to college in about two hours, and Don, hitchhiking, was right behind us. We paid a price in push-ups, a paddle, and the Miracle Mile. Not too bad considering, and Don didn't give us any shit for the rest of the semester.

By the end of the semester, our class was beginning to bond and the stress of hazing turned out to be more in the mind than in the muscles. Over the summer we were to make a pledge paddle to present to our big brother at the beginning of Hell Week.

During that semester and for the rest of college most of us drank more than we should have. We played drinking games and the beer flowed, but I don't remember ever seeing anyone being forced to drink. It was mostly beer, because it was cheap, and if you couldn't hold it, a trip to the toilet or the bushes was necessary.

The good thing about beer is you don't die from drinking too much. It has a low alcohol content and you throw up long before you die. Unlike hard liquor, with a high alcohol content that can cause death, if you binge drink. Beer was cheap, so that is what we drank. Thank God.

It was not, however, all fun and games. The saddest thing possible happen on a Saturday night in the winter of second semester. Arv Anderson and Don Gikas had driven their dates back to Centenary in Arv's car. They had had too much to drink and on the way back, on a two lane section of Route 24 in New Jersey, Arv drove across the center line and hit another car head on. Arv was killed immediately and Don (everyone called him Gikas) was taken to the hospital in Phillipsburg, NJ. We all gave blood that Sunday, I almost passed out at the size of the needle, but Gikas died that night. The two people in the other car were badly hurt, but fortunately survived.

Arv and Gikas were both sophomores and if you could have picked the best of their class, or any class, they both would have been at the top of the list. They were smart, good looking, and had a confidence beyond their years. You might even have said "future presidents," and I don't mean only of the fraternity. It was a true tragedy. A few of the brothers went to their funerals. The loss was profound and the next weekend the college, mostly Chi Phi, was still gripped in sorrow. It didn't last. We didn't learn from this lesson. By the following weekend, things were essentially back to normal. Fortunately, we never paid this price again, for what was clearly similar reckless behavior.

A word about sports in college, since they were so important to me in high school. I was a good athlete in high school in several sports, but average at the college level -- even at Lafayette which wasn't exactly a farm system for the pros. I should have played football, but because it started when you arrived in the fall, I was afraid I couldn't both play and keep up my grades. A wise decision in the end. I just wasn't good enough at basketball, so that was out. Rich played basketball his freshman year, but not after that.

I was well-coordinated and big enough to play college sports (6'1" and 190 lbs.), but I hadn't been well-coached in high school and was just average in speed and strength. My main advantage was my 6th sense for whatever game we were playing. Better than most other players in high school ball, I could sense the other team's weaknesses, anticipate where things were going, and be there to take advantage. This often made me look better than I was, but in college most everyone had some form of 6th sense and that was when my lack of speed and strength was exposed. You might think it was difficult for me to accept a realistic assessment of my athletic abilities, but it wasn't. I was just happy it worked so well in high school, when I most needed confidence building.

By the spring, I had decided to give baseball a try given that I had a better idea of the impact it would have on my grades. This was always my plan, especially since the head coach was Charlie Gilbert. Charlie was the shortstop on the St. Louis Cardinal's "Gas House Gang" team that won two World Series. He was considered one of the best coaches in the country and routinely took Lafayette to the college World Series.

Sadly, Charlie died suddenly in the winter of my freshmen year. They moved the freshmen baseball coach to varsity while they looked for a new head coach, and had the wrestling coach take on the freshmen baseball team. Oh joy.

As practices started in early March, in freezing weather, I felt a glimmer of hope in that the freshman class seemed not destined to make the World Series. Two of the best players were engineers on academic probation, so the possibility of play increased. That was the good news. The bad news was the two remaining best players were the shortstop and third baseman. These were the two positions I wanted to play. Not thinking it was good for me to volunteer to play any position, I became the fifth infielder. This created two problems. First, you sat on the bench during the early innings in miserable 40-degree weather, shaking most of the time. Second, I was used to being the star and sitting on the bench was a considerable shock to my ego. One good thing, no one, and I mean no one, came to see our games. I suffered quietly, out of the public eye.

Along about the 5ᵗʰ inning when we were losing, I usually got a chance to pinch hit and play the infield. Unfortunately, by this time I was shivering and my hands were blocks of ice. These were the days long before batting gloves.

Despite all this, by the 6ᵗʰ game I was batting almost .500, as I had only gotten up about 10 times, but had 5 hits and an amazing 4 RBIs, the most on the team. Now truth be said, not all of my hits were screaming line drives. Most were ground balls between first and second or bloopers between the infield and outfield. Nevertheless, I got up with men on base and got the job done, if not in heroic fashion.

All during this time, Rich was covering baseball for the school newspaper and gave me a lot of ink, even when it wasn't deserved. He made it seem that I was hitting line drives. Bless him.

Most of our games were during the week. For away games, we boarded busses at noon with our uniforms on and drove for hours to the opponent's field. We played the game, got back on the bus for the ride home in the dark, showered in the locker room, got dinner, and went to the library to study. Not exactly the big leagues.

Some of our games were on Saturday, which were much better than the weekdays. After a month or so, when the coach could not continue to ignore me, I had to miss one of the weekend games to go to Judy Atchison's wedding. I was actually in the wedding and it was important to my mother that I go. I told the coach the story, but I guess this was something a baseball/wrestling coach could not understand.

The game after the wedding was with Rutgers and the coach had promised I would start as shortstop. When we got to Rutgers and found out the opposing pitcher was a lefty, I was told I wasn't starting because I batted lefthanded. The theory held that lefties couldn't hit lefties. Wrong. I learned to bat against a great lefty, Danny Dipilito, in the back yard.

So I sat on the bench again until late in the game when we were behind. Finally, I got my chance. I knew I could hit this guy and waited for my pitch. With the first swing I hit a line drive foul behind first base. Good contact and I was ever more confident. The next pitch was the one I wanted, but missed by an inch and popped up to the second baseman. It's no exaggeration to say that that at-bat ended my baseball career.

Truth be told, I was not that good and there were so many other interesting things to do that I didn't miss playing. Inter-fraternity sports were just my speed, fun to play, and I never looked back.

Everything said and done, I was pleased to have gotten through freshman year with a C+ GPA and soon to be a brother of Chi Phi, even though my sports career was over. I would have normally gone back to camp for the summer, but because of Dad's death, I wanted to be home. Also Pastor Carl wasn't coming back as director and they had hired a real jerk. Phil didn't like him and I knew I wouldn't, but I was sad not to be with Phil and Ellen for another summer. They understood why.

14.

SUMMER OF 1966, CONSTRUCTION WORK

MOM WORKED FOR A lawyer, Hugh Savoy, who did real estate work and represented a local developer of high-end single family homes. Through this connection, I got a job with a mason who worked on the new homes. It was a small family business. Three Portuguese masons: the boss, and two others. There were also two Puerto Rican guys. One was senior, the foreman, and related by marriage to one of the masons. The other guy was a laborer like me. I was low man on the totem pole and was assigned the worst work. But compared to camp, the wages were terrific. Little did I know how hard I would work for the money.

Charlie, the owner of the gas station at the end of Union Avenue, knew me since I was 3 years old and gave me an old jalopy to get back and forth to work. It saved my life. We worked all over Bergen County, NJ and started at 7 am.

We worked from 7 to 4:30 and half day on Saturday. And I mean we worked!! Since they didn't work through the winter, they had to make hay when the sun was shining. We took a break about 9:30 and essentially ate a full meal, then again at lunch. Our break was only as long as it took to eat and then back to work, maybe 15 minutes. Most of the time we were building cinder block foundations or laying the brick work for the houses and the chimneys. They were all single-family homes, some pretty big.

My first day we were pouring footings, which required wheel barrel work to get the concrete from the truck to the forms. I got serious blisters that day and almost spilled a load or two. I think I would have been fired if I had lost a load, and wasn't sure how I performed. The masons didn't talk too much and when they did it was either Portuguese or Spanish. I got home, ate dinner, and went to bed.

The whole idea was to make sure that the two masons, sometimes three if the boss worked, were supplied with the materials they needed so they didn't waste any time. This was mostly cinder blocks, bricks and mortar. I was in charge of the cinder blocks and bricks, and my sidekick was responsible for the mortar. The foreman didn't pull his weight in my opinion. We didn't need too much management oversight, but he seemed to think we did. He was also fond of the coffee and beer runs.

The masons could work fast, and you had to keep up. We had a small cement mixer that could keep the masons supplied with mortar, providing it didn't break down. Mixing by hand was out of the question. The other laborer ran the mixer and got the mortar to the masons in a wheel barrel. It was the foreman's job to make sure the mixer didn't break down and there was enough cement and sand to stoke the machine. It did break once, and the boss chewed him a new asshole. I enjoyed every minute.

The bags of cement and sand came on flatbed trucks with the blocks and bricks. Everything was unloaded on pallets as close as possible to the house. Unfortunately, the only way to move cinder blocks or bricks to where they were needed was by brute force. My brute force. I got my first lesson when we were building a foundation with 12-inch blocks, the largest size. Blocks came in 8, 10 and 12 inch sizes, and most foundations were built with 10 inch blocks. This was a big house and hence the large size. The blocks for the top course were called semi-solid. That ment the three holes were half-filled, which made each block especially heavy compared to the normal blocks where the holes were open.

I quickly realized that you needed gloves to move cinder blocks, or your fingertips were shredded. Gloves solved the problem but didn't make the blocks lighter. I lifted up my first semi-solid 12-inch block and, finding it quite heavy, began to carry one down to the foundation where the masons were soon to need it. The boss came by as I returned for my second block. He motioned that I was doing it all wrong, and at first I thought how nice it was for him to give me some advice to make my life easier. His advice was to pick up two blocks, one in each hand, a suggestion that had two results. First, it balanced the weight which made walking easier, but doubled the pain. Second, it doubled my production and reduced the likelihood that the masons would run out of blocks to lay.

That day was brutal, but I got used to it, and mercifully, there weren't too many more 12-inch semi-solid blocks that summer.

This was the summer of 1966, the hottest on record. Concrete highways in NYC buckled in the heat and were shut down. A definition or two might help: cement is the gray powder that comes in 90-pound bags. Cement is mixed with sand and water to make mortar, and gravel is added to make concrete. It's the concrete that was expanding in the heat and buckling on the highways.

There were state labor rules that said we shouldn't work on roofs when the temperature was higher than 90 degrees. This happened often in the afternoon that summer, but never stopped us from working. Some of the mini mansions had several chimneys. Once above the roof line, this required getting the mortar and bricks up a ladder onto the roof right next to the mason working on the chimney. Lightheadedness often accompanied the walk on the roof, but fortunately never resulted in a fall.

There was a tool that helped carry red brick. Five or six bricks were set side by side and you rested the tool on top. As you picked up the handle, it closed two clamps, one at each end, and the pressure held the bricks together as you moved them. I dropped a load on a roof once, but I recovered and didn't lose a brick.

Breaking a brick or block was not a good idea. Early in the summer, I dropped a cinder block near one of the mansions and it landed on a small rock I didn't see. It cracked in half. My first reaction was, "so what, it's only one of many." The boss had a different reaction. He had paid for every one of the blocks and breaking one lost him money. This was explained quite clearly, and I didn't forget it for one moment for the rest of the summer. I think I only lost one more all summer.

As I worked into the system and they saw I was at least trying, one of the masons started to treat me like a human being. He would give me small pieces of advice about how to avoid the boss's wrath. The boss was not mean, he was a man of few words, and he focused on what I was doing wrong and not on what I was doing right. I respected him; he was running a business and was a tough cookie.

After lunch every day, the two masons and the boss would break out the Miller High Life. They had several beers and never slowed down or miss-laid a brick. I rarely had one and if I did it was at the very end of the day. With the heat, I would have passed out if I started to drink right after lunch.

I learned the trade and a few times during a break, one of the masons would hand me the towel and let me lay a block or brick. He usually took it apart and re-laid it, but I was getting the hang of it. They were very talented masons and took pride in their work, even if most of it was going to be buried.

I didn't miss a day all summer, but one Saturday I was late after a night out with the boys. When I arrived, I immediately started moving bricks and mentioned to my mason buddy that I was hung over. By way of advice, he said never to admit to the boss why I was late, just start working. The boss didn't give a shit why you were late, he only cared that it affected business. I certainly didn't get paid for that hour I didn't work.

I had one happy lunch break. We were working on a house the same time that two carpenters and their helper, also a college kid, were framing the first floor. I was sitting next to the foundation eating lunch and they were not far away, but out of sight on the first floor. I could hear them talking when the helper asked them why I made 2 dollars an hour more than he did. They laughed and said: "Take a look at what he does, he earns it. You have it easy." My chest expanded and after a few minutes, walked to the curb and happily carried TWO 12-inch semi-solid cinder blocks back to the foundation.

It was a hard summer, with very few nights out. I worked my ass off and slept like the dead. If I didn't already realize, this was a stark lesson on why a college education was the right way to go.

I ended work a few days early, so I could take a short vacation to the Hamptons. This was not jet setting to some mansion, as you will see. I drove out with Rich Kletter to meet one of his friends who was working at a summer camp. Daryl, Rich's friend, was to provide us a place to sleep.

We got an early start and arrived about 1 pm after tracking down Daryl. We went to the beach, had a hotdog and beer, and looked for an open spot on the sand in close proximity to as many girls as possible. Daryl went back to work and we just hung around.

My last day of work had been the day before and I was content to just rest and do nothing. I had a good tan from the waist up, but white legs. I must have looked funny, but that didn't last long as my legs got burned under the afternoon sun. A few more beers and we wandered back to find Daryl, and where we were going to sleep. The good news was we had a place, but the bad news was there was only one bed and one blanket. I won the coin toss and took the bed. Rich got the floor and the blanket.

Now, at a summer camp you would think another blanket could be found more easily than a bed, so that is why I took the bed. The extra blanket was never found and it was a cool night. Turns out that wasn't my only problem. After a cheap dinner washed down with many more beers, we went to a local bar with a band. It was hopping. All the pretty girls we didn't see on the beach had arrived at this watering hole. It was like being a kid in a candy store.

I danced up a storm with several girls and was having the time of my life. Unfortunately, the beer was catching up with me and the dancing, which normally sobered me up, wasn't working. I knew things were turning bad in the middle of a song, so I just walked out into the parking lot, stumbled to the end of a row of cars, and blew dinner. It wasn't pretty, but it solved the problem. I tried to miss but got part of a bumper. That too wasn't pretty.

I took a few deep breaths and gamely walked back into the dance hall. My first stop was the men's room to splash some water on my face and to see what I looked like. Not bad, considering. However, I was not quite as dashing the rest of the night and we all went home empty-handed. In hindsight it might have had something to do with my breath, which unfortunately the bathroom mirror had no comment on.

Badly drunk, I had a miserable, cold night, sunburned and all. We got up early, had breakfast, and headed home. So much for the Hamptons. Haven't been back since.

14.

SOPHOMORE YEAR

THE BEGINNING OF SOPHOMORE year was Hell Week. This was the week before classes started, and culminated in Hell Night and your induction into the Chi Phi Fraternity brotherhood. The week was a bonding time with your fellow classmates/pledges while you fixed up the house (painting, cleaning, and minor repairs), all the while harassed by the brothers. The worst part was sleeping on the floor in a quiet spot where you wouldn't get stepped on.

Hell Week was really about Hell Night, a tradition that had been refined over many years and today would be considered outrageous by the politically correct, which sadly includes most liberal arts professors. In fact, if they had experienced a small dose of Hell Night, they might have a broader, healthier outlook on life. You be the judge.

The details of Hell Night are shrouded in mystery, as brothers are not to speak of them except in hushed tones of dread. This tests your mental abilities to calibrate the risks (read: fear) with your trust that the brothers will not do anything too crazy. You are internally fearful that you will not live up to the tradition but comforted by the fact that all the upper classmen have gone through it, seemingly none the worse for wear. Nevertheless, of the 23 pledges in my class, one didn't show up for Hell Night, a mere several hours short of brotherhood. The mind can play some nasty tricks.

Hell Night starts at nightfall, no surprise there. Darkness magnifies the fear of the unknown. So does nakedness, so we all had to strip down to our undies. We found out, long before Bill Clinton was asked, who wore boxers and who wore briefs. For the night to come, boxers were preferred, fortunately my choice.

There were push-ups, crawling through mazes, more push-ups, drinking slimy concoctions, and lots of yelling by the brothers. This was pretty routine harassment; the real tension came from the fact that you were by yourself and the brothers were constantly yelling that you were falling behind your fellow pledges, and not performing to the high standards that the Brotherhood required for initiation. Pure bullshit, but again the mind is vulnerable, especially when you are isolated and under stress.

The real fun and juvenile creativity were reserved for the basement and the last two stations. The second to last station was in the TV room. Everything was cleared to the sides, with one chair in the middle and a large target opposite the chair against one wall. You were told to "drop trow" and stand on the chair, buck naked. A brother, sporting a scowl, approached; in my case, it was Bob Rufe. He held a hammer and a 15-foot length of string, one end of which was securely attached to the hammer and the other was tied as a noose.

As you were handed the noose end of the string, you began to grasp what the instruction might be. Sure enough, you were told to secure the noose around your dick. With wide eyes you clumsily followed instructions, desperately trying to figure out how to avoid the next step. This was a rare occasion when a little prick was an advantage.

You were then handed the hammer and TOLD to throw it with great vigor at the target, 16 feet away, and that if you didn't hit the target the first time you would get a second try. Now this is where your faith in the brotherhood faced the ultimate test. Frantically trying to figure out the "trick," for surely there was a trick -- or was there? Were the brothers crazy enough to be serious?

Not having the presence of mind to figure it out, after having been worn down over the previous several hours, I gave in to blind faith and threw the hammer. It definitely was not my fast ball, but just made the target. My faith was rewarded. The string harmlessly broke before my dick was dragged across the floor, too much laughter by the brothers in attendance. The string had been previously broken and attached with candle wax, which was not detected by me or anyone else in the heat of battle. With a nervous giggle, I moved to the last station in the Rock Room. A blindfold was attached as you entered the back of the room away from the bar.

The Rock Room, with so much history, was the appropriate venue for the finale. Still naked, they started by sliding you down the center table made slippery by some magic goo. As long as you avoided splinters, it was a fine ride, with brothers pushing and screaming all around. At the end between the table and the bar was a bathtub filled with water. You were maneuvered into the tub, with your head above water and blindfold attached.

At this point things got very quiet for a moment until one of the brothers in a very solemn tone informed you that there was one final question you needed to answer correctly. This was it, one correct answer and you were a brother. Another long silence and then the question was "popped." Have you ever masturbated? For most, present company included, it was an easy answer. It was not a trick question. You said yes, got dunked, and were proudly made a brother. There were those, mostly good Catholics, who needed to be dunked many times before admitting the obvious. Watching this drama unfold was great fun and an insightful lesson in human nature.

No one ever got hurt, and everyone, I mean everyone, learned a bit more about themselves that night. Things you don't learn in a classroom and that stay with you for a lifetime. I'm not big on rituals, but this one was a valuable life lesson and it's a shame it's been discontinued.

After the adventure of Hell Week and Hell Night, things settled down to the routine of classes. All engineering students still took the same classes sophomore year. First semester was calculus, physics with a lab, strength of materials, thermodynamics, and Social Darwinism was my elective. I got off to a terrific start with good enough grades in the first round of exams to make the Dean's List mid-semester.

I spent time in the library seriously trying to understand differential equations. This is a key part of calculus, essentially invented by Isaac Newton. It's fundamental in understanding and predicting how things change. Very little in life is "steady state," in position and/or velocity. Stuff, like rockets, move around. They are pushed by engines and pulled by gravity and friction, among other things. Calculus helps predict how a rocket will perform under these different pushes and pulls, or what will be the rate of change of the rocket in flight. It's safe to say that we would not have landed on the Moon without calculus. Needless to say, it's critical to much in engineering and I gave my best to understand the concepts, at least at first.

The other ball-buster course was Thermodynamics. This can also be traced in part to Newton's genus and deals with energy, mostly in terms of heat. It also deals with the lack of order in a system, or the gradual decline of a system into disorder. There are several laws in Thermodynamics, the second being: entropy is always increasing with time. I'm still not sure what entropy means, so you can guess how well I did in this class, as things gradually declined into disorder. I had to pass the final exam to pass the course and I did an all-nighter studying. We had four or five questions on the final and I was working hard filling out the answers, as I understood them, in my Blue Book. We were in a classroom and Jack Sherry was sitting next to me, a short 12 inches away. I paused, looked up, and couldn't help but notice that Jack was clearly answering one of the questions wrong in his Blue Book. I didn't know how to give him a heads-up without being accused of cheating, so I kicked him in the foot and went on with my work. I passed. I don't remember if Jack did or not, but if he did, I should have gotten an assist.

A word about Social Darwinism. I had to have a non-engineering elective, so I signed up for this class not knowing what it was going to be about. I knew of Darwin and thought there might be some biology involved, which I liked. Of course it was taught in the philosophy department, far from the biology building, which should have given me some pause about my initial assumption. It was about using Darwin's theory of natural selection to support the concept of a superior race, the white race. It was big in the later 19th century and sadly is still with us. A sick, hateful social perversion of the most consequential natural law formulated by man.

Most of what happened in the classroom is lost to me, but as a newly minted brother of Chi Phi on the Dean's List, I thought my shit didn't stink. What I failed to realize was that mid-term grades were based on only about one-third of the course work.

I stopped taking classes seriously and took full advantage of the pleasures of Chi Phi. Just before the end of the semester I realized I was in deep shit, the kind that stinks, but it was too late. My final grades crashed, I flunked physics, and was on academic probation. I particularly disliked physics lab on Thursday mornings from 8 to 11, but strangely passed the lab so I only needed to re-take the classroom part. Small consolation. I re-took it my senior year and passed.

I met with my advisor and he asked what happened. I couldn't tell him it was the Rock Room, so I simply said I would do better. Worse than that was reporting the sorry results to Mother at Christmas break. She didn't say much but I knew what she was thinking. I had a rare opportunity to go to college that she and my dad never had and I was screwing it up and blowing my future. It was a wake-up call and although I never got close to the Dean's List again, I made sure to graduate to make Mom proud.

I don't remember too many details of that fall semester but did spend a lot of time in the Rock Room. I also took lots of afternoon naps and cut a lot of classes, especially ROTC. What a bore. I had good intentions of only napping for 30 minutes, waking refreshed, and hitting the books with some enthusiasm. Unfortunately, I would wake up, turn over, and sleep on.

One thing that caused the naps was our 10 pm bridge game in the coffee shop in the dark basement of Hogg Hall. Hogg was right next to our dorm (I didn't live in the fraternity house until senior year) and my roommate Skip and I met with Dennis Henderson and Tom

Bradshaw (all fraternity brothers) to play bridge from 10 to midnight. Tom and I played Dennis and Skip. It was a wonderful get together but cut studying short.

One other change in sophomore year was interfraternity sports. These were intense, both for bragging rights and because there were many good players, who like me, didn't make, or were not interested in, varsity sports. There were also varsity athletes who couldn't play because they were on academic probation. The net result was good games played hard.

We played flag football, where you wore a belt with three flags attached with Velcro. To stop the play (tackle) you needed to grab a flag from the guy with the ball. This avoided major collisions and injuries, but took some getting used to, since you could actually run into the guy with the ball, but if you missed the flag, you lost! One of the upper classman was a quarterback in HS, like me, and had claims on that position. I was not about to contest this, so played any available position. We had fun, especially after I figured out how to grab flags. I got a few lumps in this process.

I also played on the basketball and softball teams. I did quite well and it was a great outlet for my interest in sports. However, as I moved onto junior and senior years, I got fat and out of shape and lost some interest in participating. I would bring a beer and root for the good guys.

One of the reasons I lost interest was the Rock Room. Much of my time in the Rock Room was spent first learning and then playing Wales Tails. A great drinking game you can play with three or more people, although five or six work best. One person starts by saying "Wales Tails Prince of Wales stationary point at (pick a number) calls on (pick another number)." Say six people are playing. If you start you are the 'stationary' point. If you pick three for the first (stationary) number everyone else has to figure out their number in relation to you. Starting to your right it would be 4, 5, 6, 1, 2, and back to you (3). If you call on 5 for the second number, that would be the second person to the right of the stationary 3. If you are in the 5 position, you need to immediately begin the game again, picking a new stationary point, etc. This is repeated until someone can't follow the numbers and therefore can't respond or responds incorrectly. This sin is washed away by a drink of beer. Only a drink, not the whole glass. We wanted to play for more than 15 minutes, and sometimes we did for hours.

Partly because of the name, I loved this game and don't think I have ever seriously played another drinking game. I did get good at Wales Tails, but everyone loses his fair share. And it was mostly guys playing in a fraternity at an all-male college. Over the years there were a few accomplished women players, Kathy Flannery being one of the best in my recollection.

Actually, I almost didn't get to graduation because of Wales Tails, but I'll get to that later.

One night I was in the Rock Room and having a bad time at Wales Tails. In frustration I knocked off my glasses and broke the frame. I went upstairs to see if anyone had a spare pair with a prescription even close to mine. Someone gave me a pair of sunglasses that helped a bit. I returned to the game. Shortly after returning, Wayne Gilbert came in, saw me with the sunglasses, and immediately called me Ray Moore. After, of course, Ray Charles, except he said it as one word. Raymoore. For some reason it stuck and today some brothers still call me that.

Because of my low GPA and the physics disaster, Christmas in Vermont with Leslie and Henry was a bit glum. Henry was teaching at UVM and Leslie was taking care of Jill, who was 1 year old. I thought it was pretty cool that my sister had a baby girl.

One day Mother took charge of Jill, with great joy, and Leslie and I went skiing at Bolton Valley, a small mountain near Stow. We had a lesson since neither of us had ever been on skis. We were the only ones in the class and soon found out that the instructor was one of Henry's students at UVM. We, especially Leslie, got a special lesson. After the lesson, Leslie went to the bar, but I headed for the chair lift. I wanted to get my money's worth. It was about 5 degrees, but sunny and no wind. After working through the lesson and getting warmed up, I thought the weather was fine, and it was.

I stumbled off the chair lift and made one run down the beginner slope, mostly trying to slow down using the snow-plow method. On the second run, I increased the speed just in time to hit one of the many icy patches on the mountain. It was too late. The skies slipped off the ice and I went down...hard. As I tried to break the fall, my arms got tangled up in the poles and I hit the ice hip first. I was overcome with pain and thought my hip was in pieces. Fortunately, not. I hobbled back to the lodge, had a strong drink or two, and have never again been on downhill skis.

Back to school and my first January Rush Week as a brother. I was pretty good at slinging the bullshit, and we got an exceptionally good class of pledges. Actually it was easy selling Chi Phi, despite a few dry years in the mid 1960s. My freshman year, there were only two senior Chi Phis. It was the end of a poor period of recruitment, I know not why. The house started to re-build after that and the two years ahead of us were strong, with 20 to 25 brothers in each class. My pledge class was over 20.

It was hard for me to imagine why Chi Phi wasn't always strong, especially because the house, Vallamont, was amazing and it had the Rock Room, famous throughout the Lehigh Valley. Of course, there were 20-odd other fraternities, some having equally nice houses, competing for freshmen pledges. Reputation was all important, and that changed from time to time. Also, since over 80 percent of the students joined a fraternity, there was one for almost everyone, but the competition was keen to get good pledges.

After Rush Week, classes started and the routine began, with one exception. I was now determined to keep my grades above water. For some reason I was allowed to take the second semester of Physics, despite flunking the first. I passed. I also took another semester of calculus, dynamics, thermodynamics, and religion. The religion was a wonderful class taught by a great professor. It was about the seven major religions of the world and I wish I could take it again and pay more attention. I had a gentleman C+ average, about 2.5 GPA, and was pleased with myself. Keeping out of academic trouble was the name of the game.

On the social side, I had been dating Alayne from Camp Beisler days, through my freshmen year, which was her senior year in HS. She went to Cedar Crest, where Leslie went, right down Route 22 in Allentown. At first, this seemed too good to be true, but we grew apart during the first semester of my sophomore year. I believe this was partly due to the drinking that seemed ever present in fraternity life. It wasn't that she didn't enjoy a good party, but the intensity and absence of other forms of entertainment was a bit much.

It was also true that despite my inner doubts and anxieties, I apparently projected the image of the person who Tom Wolfe would later call a "Master of the Universe." This was master with a small m, but nevertheless I was self-centered, felt entitled, and had an arrogant streak that wasn't enormously attractive. I'm sure Alayne felt that she didn't come first in the things I valued, even though she did.

In the fall, each home football game was a party weekend. This included a casual party on Friday night, a cocktail party after the football game at the house on Saturday, followed by dinner in town and a dance with a live band back at the House in the evening. In the spring, with no football, there were still four or five party weekends with different themes.

If it wasn't a party weekend, dates were not so important. If you had a date, there was usually a party in someone's room, or the Rock Room, and things were casual. On party weekends, having a date was much more important in the social scheme of things. You were sort of expected to have a date and things were more formally organized.

Actually, one party weekend Bill McConahue and I were stood up by our dates on Thursday, just before the weekend. It was not Alayne. Some other girl, who might have been a blind date. As I remember it, we were all sitting down to dinner Thursday night as Bill Koch took the fateful call. He proceeded to the dining room and announced in a booming voice that Bill and Rick had been stood up. Everyone laughed. Not a good experience for confidence building. I drowned my sorrows for two days in the Rock Room.

One party weekend in February or March, Alayne came over from Cedar Crest on a Friday night and the party began. Actually, it was a continuation from Thursday night, the usual start of the weekend. It was clear I had a head start and she didn't appreciate it, with good reason. All of a sudden, she was gone and I had no idea where she went. These were the days before cell phones. With some help from the few folks who were sober, it became clear she had left the house for points unknown.

I was embarrassed that she had left me, which in my self-centered world was a blow to my ego. I left the house to avoid awkward questions, but with no thought of what to do next. I wandered across campus and into a bar on the hill, not for another beer, but to have a hamburger and sober up. Actually, I wasn't old enough to get another beer to cry in, so I got a Coke.

After inhaling the hamburger in 30 seconds and burping several times, I felt better. Then I headed back to the House to find Alayne. I was not optimistic. It was dark, cold, and I suspected she had gotten a ride back to Cedar Crest with some other girls. There were typically lots of Cedar Crest girls on campus each weekend, but especially a designated party weekend.

As I was walking in front of South College, I saw Alayne walking toward me. She was easy to pick out under the streetlights and there was no one else around. I mustered up an apology and convinced her to walk with me back to the house to find a ride back to Cedar Crest as soon as possible. Once accomplished, this began about a year when we went our separate ways.

The big spring party weekend occurred in late April and tradition called for a venue off campus in the Poconos. More effort went into getting a date for this weekend than any other. Securing one indicated you could convince some lovely lady to accompany you to a deserted resort where there were a lot more double beds than single ones.

With Alayne gone, I got lucky with a blind date from the Allentown Nursing School, rounded up by Kathy, who later became Jim Flannery's wife. We had a party at the house on Friday night, they went back to Allentown, and we reconvened on Saturday morning for the drive to the Poconos. Someone had a car, maybe Kathy.

The resort was past its glory days and this was the off season. We got good rates. My date and I were assigned a cabin, as sophomores we were low in the pecking order. The upper classmen got the better rooms in the main building.

We started drinking at lunch and never stopped. My date was a trooper and kept up with the best of us. After dinner a band played until 11 pm, when the parties moved into individual rooms and cabins. We made the rounds and finally, in the wee hours, decided to head back to our cabin.

The most direct route was from the cabin we left, across a field to our cabin. We stumbled through the field with the music fading in the background. The weeds were high, so we helped each other thinking only of bed. Sex was out of the question in our condition. We just wanted to pass out, which we did after taking off most of our clothes and climbing under the sheets.

We slept like babies, only to wake to the morning sun and serious headaches. We slowly started to get feeling in our bodies and get up. We couldn't move because our legs were stuck to the sheets, which were blood red. We were both shocked until we figured out what had happened. It became apparent that I had dragged my date through a briar patch coming back to the cabin. I had pants on, but she didn't. Her pain the night before had been deadened by the alcohol, but it had not stopped the blood. Our legs were stuck to the sheets by dried blood, in a scene out of "Psycho."

She needed to get into the shower and run warm water to soften the blood and disentangle the sheets. After we got over the fright, we cleaned up, had breakfast in the main dining hall, and headed back to college in the first car available. God knows what the cleaning staff thought about the crimson bed sheets. We were out of there! All in all, we had a good time, but I never saw her again.

16.

SUMMER OF 1967, GAS STATION WITH PHIL AND ELLEN

I HAD WORKED FOR the mason and lived home the summer after my freshman year. This was to spend time with Mom, and oh, by the way, I was paid very well for my sweat. All this time I had kept in touch with Phil and Ellen. It just so happened they were leaving Camp Beisler to run a gas station in Hackettstown, NJ. Phil was also building a house in Budd Lake. I had helped Phil a bit on the house during winter weekends and he asked if I would help him run the gas station in the summer. I would live with them in the Budd Lake house. I liked this idea, and Mom did as well. Phil and Ellen were the best and I got along with their kids, Linda and Steven. Steven was a handful, but still too young to cause much trouble. That would change later.

Charlie, who owned the gas station up the street in Cresskill, again gave me a used car to get around. He liked my mother (everyone did) and it was a blessing. It was a big Oldsmobile and there was something wrong with the steering. The power steering worked turning left, but it took two men and a boy to turn right. I was thrilled. I was getting free room and board at Phil and Ellen's and a free car from Charlie.

The gas station was a Phillips 66, not a common name in New Jersey in the 1960s. Phil didn't care. He said it was all about service, since it was essentially the same gas in all the stations. If you gave good service, people would come back. The station was on Route 46 just east of downtown Hackettstown, NJ.

Since this was before I-80, Route 46 was the main east/west route between North Jersey/NYC and the Pocono Mountains. So during the summer there were traffic jams in front of the station every Friday going west and ones on Sunday going east. This was good for pumping lots of gas, but the way to make money was to have regular local customers and do their engine work. This meant oil changes, tune-ups, brakes, tires, alternators, fuel pumps, and generally fixing problems.

Phillips 66 wanted to pump lots of gas, but you made less than a penny on each gallon. The benefits from pumping gas came from discounts in other areas. Depending on how much you pumped, there were discounts on the utility costs of operating the station. The other utility discount came from keeping the station open at least 18 hours a day. This was significant, so Phil wanted to stay open even though we didn't do much business after 9 p.m.

The plan was for Phil to open the station at 6 a.m. and work until 6 p.m. I arrived at noon and closed the station at midnight. This was seven days a week during the summer. When I went back to college, Phil hired someone to help and the station closed earlier. Besides, he needed some time off and 18 hours during the winter didn't make much sense even given the utility discount.

Pumping gas of course went on all day and otherwise you worked on the cars in the bays. We didn't always have work in the bays, so we sat around or kept the place clean. It always seemed like we either had nothing to do, or we were going crazy. If the two of us were there, we could handle most anything, but with one person it was tense if four cars all wanted gas at the same time and you were working on a car in one of the bays with the owner looking over your shoulder. Customers who were in a hurry in those situations were the worst part of the job. Some were real assholes.

Ellen kept the books and brought us lunch and dinner. We ate well but were constantly interrupted by customers. As at camp, Phil taught me all about fixing cars. Engines in those days were simple compared to the computer guided ones of today. The standard oil change or tune-up was pretty straightforward. The biggest challenges were figuring out what the problem was when someone had a broken down car. I liked working on cars. It made the time go by and by the end of the summer, I knew my way around most cars.

We had a tow truck so we could pick up a stranded car or fix one that drove in. We had two bays so could work on two cars at the same time. If need be, we both worked extra to get the cars finished. Sometimes with older cars things didn't go so well, new parts didn't fit, or access around the engine was difficult. Phil always stuck with it and got it fixed. Being able to lift the car on hydraulic lifts helped with the access issues.

A few stories. One day an elderly woman (at least to me) came in and wanted four new tires. I was thrilled with the business and in no time, she had her new tires. When I rang up the bill, she confessed she was a bit short on cash and suggested I take her engagement and wedding rings as collateral. I was dumbstruck and felt it would be terrible to take the nice lady's rings. After all she said she lived down the street and was getting her paycheck the following day. Our money would be coming shortly.

When I told Phil, he rolled his eyes and said good luck on that. He rarely got pissed off at others and of course he was right. After a few days, I got pissed at my gullibility and wanted to re-possess the tires. Phil said not to worry and to learn from my mistakes. Given the large financial implications, this illustrated why I learned so much from him.

Another time a guy, a regular customer, drove in with his 1957 Cadillac and informed us that he and his family were moving to California. They had two cars and wanted to sell the Cadillac. He asked me if I was interested at $75. Now remember, I had the Olds, but it turned out to have more problems than just the steering and I was always fixing something. So I was interested but didn't want to buy another lemon, even though owning a Caddy was a cool idea.

Phil pointed out that the four tires alone were worth about $75 dollars, and that we could keep it running. The guy was smart enough to bring it to a gas station to sell. The deal was done and I became the proud owner of a '57 Caddy, with fins as big as a 727s and a backseat big enough to house a family of four.

I took Linda and Steven to NYC in the Caddy to see the sights and felt like a big wheel when I parked the car. One night I was going home after midnight up the long hill on Route 46 just east of the station. The road was divided on what was about a 2-mile hill, two lanes in each direction, with a wooded median 500 to 1,000 feet wide in places. About halfway up, the fuel pump crapped out and I lost power. I was in the left passing lane with no one in sight, rapidly slowing down. With the last bit of forward momentum, I pulled the car off the road, but not entirely. The ass end, fins and all, was hanging out in the fast lane.

What to do? I hightailed it back to the station almost a mile away, but all downhill. I didn't want to wake Phil, so fired up the Olds and headed back to the scene of the crime. Luckily, no one had stopped, or worse, run into the back end of the Caddy, least of all a cop. I stopped right behind the Caddy, got out, and quickly got into the Caddy and put it in neutral. Then I got back into the Olds and slowly pushed the Caddy off the road. This would have been a simple task, except for the fact that the ground sloped steeply downhill into the trees that separated the east- and westbound roadways. Once the Caddy got off the road, it started to pick up speed downhill toward the trees. Fortunately, I anticipated this and had a plan. I jammed on the brakes in the Olds, jumped out, ran to catch the rolling Caddy, jumped in, and hit the brakes. Disaster avoided!

I had stopped the Caddy just in time, went home, and passed out in bed from exhaustion. The next morning, we towed the Caddy back to the station and parked it... forever. We never heard from the police and I drove the Olds for the rest of the summer. Last Caddy I ever owned.

Now to the girls. There is always a story about the girls where Phil is concerned. It wasn't that Phil cheated, he was as loyal a husband as ever walked the earth. Phil just appreciated a lovely lady and was a flirt. This approach tied into Phil's whole notion of customer service. After all, if you wanted lots of local repeat customers, why not focus on the pretty ones? You see, the Phillips 66 stations were ahead of their time. They had canopies to protect from the rain and vacuum cleaners built into the islands. This allowed you to vacuum a car, even in the rain, and gain valuable service points. Of course, this took some time, and you couldn't do it for everyone. Hence the focus on the pretty girls.

For a new customer, the process started by getting the order from the driver's side window (fill it up, 5 dollars' worth, etc.). Once the gas started to pump, you washed the windshield, which we did for every car. Remember it was summer and washing the windshield, as Phil pointed out to me, often provided a leg shot (ladies only). So by this time, with views from several angles, you knew if you were going to pull the vacuum trick. But first you asked if they wanted you to check the oil. Unlike today, it was truly full service. The main advantage of a vacuum was to get the driver out of the car. Phil was convinced he could charm each lovely lady into being a lifelong customer if he got her out of the car. His preferred approach was to have me vacuum, while he was charming.

If one of us was working on a car and the vacuum came on, we knew there was a hot one getting gas. We would wander out of the bay to check things out. If it was me who wandered out of the bay, Phil would hand over the vacuum to his loyal assistant. Since Phil and I had different visions of beauty, we often had long conservations about why the lady in question might re-appeared the next day. Was it because of the short dark Italian or the tall redhead? We never resolved that issue, except in one case.

There was one very glamorous customer who re-appeared several times. Although not my type, Phil was sure she had the hots for me. I was not so sure, but he convinced me. One day, I did the vacuum trick for maybe the third time and at the end, during some small talk,

I asked if she might consider going out for a drink. She very nicely said she would love to but was married. I was speechless and never saw her again.

Now, right across the street, actually a 4-lane highway, was a Dairy Bar. It served breakfast, lunch, and dinner, and specialized in ice cream, as the name implied. We made many trips across the highway and got to know the waitresses very well. I dated one, who went to Centenary, for a short time. It was a mistake that has long been forgotten. There was another waitress, who I had a crush on, but who was unfortunately also married. They married young in western NJ.

Here again Phil, even though he knew she was married, thought she liked me. That may have been true and late in the evening when things were slow and she was working, I would go over and have some ice cream. We would have long talks at the end of the counter, until a car would pull into the station and I would race across Rt. 46 to pump some gas.

She had a young son she was wild about, but her husband, not so much. Her husband was a blue collar worker and she seemed sad to be trapped in Hackettstown without much of a future. She was wise beyond her years. I never knew if she was trying to tell me something or just blowing off some steam with the redhead from the gas station, but I was not about to be a homewrecker. I came real close a few times, she had eyes that made your knees weak and other things strong, but even I, a "Master of the Universe," knew it would be wrong, with a capital W.

In addition to the Dairy Bar, there was a real bar on Route 46 across from Budd Lake, the actual lake. It was at the top of the long hill noted earlier and essentially on my way home to Phil and Ellen's. After my ice cream at 10 pm, I would often stop at the bar after closing around 12:15 a.m. The bar was open till 1 or 2 a.m. depending on the crowd, but most of the time during the week I was the only customer.

Needless to say, I became friendly with the two bartenders, both women who shared the duty. They were much older than the waitresses at the Diary Bar. Maybe in their 30s or 40s, which to me was getting up there. I think they thought of me as a kid brother and we got along famously. After midnight there was only one bartender. Often on a slow night, the bartender would close the place as we talked and I finished my last beer.

One night as I walked to the car, my favorite bartender emerged from the side door, walked up to me, and asked if I wanted to go home with her. Now she was the good looking one and had she asked me into the back room of the bar, I would have gone in a NY second. But after my experience with married women, I didn't want to wake up in an apartment with an angry husband or boyfriend looking down at me with a shotgun. So I chickened out, made some lame excuse, and went home to sleep in the same bedroom with Steven. Likely a good decision.

I had a great summer with Phil and Ellen even though I worked crazy hours. I did conclude, however, that a gas station was not the best place to pick up nice young unmarried girls.

17.

JUNIOR YEAR

JUNIOR YEAR STARTED WITH Hell Week and Hell Night, as usual. Honestly I don't remember much of these events after my own experience. There were always enough brothers who volunteered to participate during Hell Night and make things work. I wasn't the least bit interested, so let the others get their jollies. I did spend some time observing the hammer throw and the last question in the bathtub. It was good for a few laughs, but a little went a long way.

Despite this disinterest I was elected to be co-chair of Rush Week, which was a semester away. Phil Crudden, a senior, was the other co-chair and actually the one in charge due his seniority and the fact that he was very good at whatever he did. I was thrilled to be able to work with Phil. We had two things in common, but didn't hang out together. He played baseball, a pitcher, and was very supportive of me when I played freshmen ball. He also loved the Clint Eastwood spaghetti Western movies, and I did too.

Our main job was to prepare the Pledge Book for publication. We needed to get things done before the Thanksgiving vacation to allow time for printing. I had worked on my 8th grade yearbook, but this wasn't my strong suit. Fortunately, I was in good hands, as Phil was an English major. We didn't need to start from scratch, just update the Pledge Book from the previous year. We used many of the same pictures and text.

Picking new pictures was fun, but we didn't have a great number to select from. This was way before the smartphone. We made a rule that all the pictures had to be at the house or on campus (e.g., intramural sports), but made one exception. We had a picture that was used the previous year and was sure it wasn't from Chi Phi. The thing is, it was a picture of a beautiful co-ed in a typical college setting, with some people in the background. We were smitten by the young lady and figured that if prospective pledges felt they would be rubbing elbows, or other parts, with the likes of our fair maiden, we would have a successful rush. So we left her in.

There wasn't much text and Phil did the editing. The main message was from the president, Ron Kennedy, and this changed very little from year to year. The final and most important decision was the cover. We needed a new cover each year.

One night Phil and I were organizing the changes and talking about the cover. We had lots of examples from the printer to choose from. We would take a stock cover and add color and a title to see how it might look. One of the covers had two hands in a handshake. Phil stopped at this one and after a moment of thought suggested that one hand be white and the other black. We looked at each other and knew this would be a statement that would be the talk of the campus during Rush Week.

We were so taken by the idea that we went down to the Rock Room and had a beer, rather unusual for a weeknight, even given our drinking ways. We got back together a few days later and got cold feet about Phil's daring idea. I have always regretted this cop out, but at the time we didn't feel we could make a controversial decision, that might have risked a successful Rush Week, without consulting the whole Brotherhood. These types of decisions are still with us.

The cover was very ordinary, with a big "Chi Phi" across the top. We did have a great pledge class and Phil and I took credit, with a sad feeling of a missed opportunity in the pit of our stomachs. Nationally, the Civil Rights Act had been passed and Martin Luther King was all over the news. We knew generally what was going on, but didn't typically watch the news or read newspapers. I was in my white, Chi Phi bubble and was not signing up to go protest in Washington DC, either about the Vietnam War or equal justice for black folks. I didn't understand how privileged we white guys were, and sadly took it for granted. There were activists on campus, but I didn't associate with their causes. My causes were graduation (decent grades) and a good time, not necessarily in that order.

There was one especially hot topic on campus during this time. It was whether the college should go co-ed. It seemed all the male colleges were going co-ed, even the military academies. It also seemed the majority of students wanted the change. This was illustrated in a student-wide poll, which the administration took, even though you got the feeling that the decision was already made. I didn't like the idea. I figured if we stayed all-male, we would be a 'one of a kind' college. Hence, we would get good candidates applying for admission, guys like me. I didn't like the idea of competing with women in the classroom, or anywhere else for that matter. I was proven wrong and have come to see this error of my youth.

At the end of your sophomore year, you picked an engineering major, civil engineering in my case. You now focused in that area, with most classes with one of the four civil engineering professors. The theory was that if you made it through the first two years, you were going to make it through the rest. Good news!

There were four civil engineering professors, Three had been at Lafayette for some time, and their clear emphasis was on structural engineering, especially bridges. The fourth professor was new and young and not a structural guy, but his classes were mostly taught to seniors, not juniors. The head of the department was an old-time railroad engineer, Professor DeMoyer. He was at the end of his career, born in the 19th century. Nevertheless, he was a good guy and taught us the basics. For example, the three loads you needed to account for in designing a bridge (dead load, live load, and impact).

He spent a lot of time talking about concrete and steel and the different properties of each. Concrete is good in compression and steel is good in tension. If you put them together, like you do in reinforced concrete beams, you get the best of both. As I recall, Professor DeMoyer liked steel more than concrete. He would say you can bend steel and it will not break. Bend concrete and it will fail. One of his favorite expressions, one I still use is: "in flexibility there is strength." He used the Empire State building as an example and noted that it was able to absorb the force of strong winds by bending and being flexible. If it were rigid, it would snap in a violent failure. So in civil engineering, as in life, it is better to be flexible than rigid.

Professor DeMoyer also taught a great lesson about "rounding off," especially as it relates to much of civil engineering. He would hold up his hand with his thumb and index fingers about 1/4-inch apart and say, "You only need to get this close and the trains will run just fine." His point was that unlike electrical engineering, in civil engineering we were mostly dealing with big things, like 30-foot-long, 5-foot-deep wide flange steel beams on a bridge. If a contractor was placing the beam and your calculations were 1/4-inch off, things would still work.

The message was to think hard about the big picture, focus on what matters, and don't get bogged down in precision that doesn't add to the project. Good advice, especially for consultants who ultimately have budgets and schedules to meet. Of course, the key was to understand what was important and what was not.

My advisor was one of the other two long term professors, Professor Vincent Forss. We had the standard meeting every semester, but honestly, I didn't get much out of the relationship. Likely because there wasn't much about structural engineering that got me excited. Writing this, I couldn't remember his name and had to look it up in the yearbook. That about says it all. Academically, junior year was a blur of standard structural courses. We tested concrete and steel in the lab and did lots of calculations. I did like the idea that we were dealing with real things, bridges etc., and not just theory. Translating the theory/calculations into building something was the best part of junior year.

I got Cs, and a few Bs, and felt just fine. At the same time, I was very much enjoying the fraternity life. I still lived with Skip in a dorm, but this year I was a proctor. Why I was selected I'll never know, but it didn't require any work and was a way for the school to justify a reduction in my room and board. Every little bit helped, and I was thrilled to tell Mom her check would be a bit smaller. I was also officially in Army ROTC and received a $50/month allowance. For the late 1960s this was huge and, as mentioned, paid for beer.

We ate all our meals at the house, except for Saturday dinner and Sunday. Every weeknight I would plan on getting up for breakfast the next morning. Unfortunately, when morning arrived, I just rolled over and never made it. Junior year we had a new chef and the food was quite good. The honeymoon ended senior year, but while it lasted it was good.

One Saturday night five of us climbed into Bob Rufe's car and went south along the river to a restaurant that had an all-you-could-eat buffet. They didn't make any money on us and we had a hard time fitting back into Bob's car. After a mile or two heading back, someone mentioned how much he liked the shrimp. With that, Bob reached into his coat pocket, pulled out a shrimp and said 'like another one?'. We laughed all the way home.

My memory is a bit fuzzy, but I wasn't dating Alayne much of my junior year. That created the opportunity for blind dates. Except for one or two repeats, they were forgettable. I'm sure the ladies felt the same. One winter weekend Mike Janiak came out from Cresskill for the weekend. We had blind dates from Centenary. At the end of the evening, we took two cars to meet the midnight curfew. Four to six in each car. Mike went first and I was a passenger in the second car. It was snowing quite heavily and the roads were slippery. As we headed into a long straight away on Route 24 in New Jersey, we saw flashing red lights and an accident up ahead. I was sure it was Mike and could only think of the crash that took Arv and Gikas on the same road my freshman year. We slowed to see the details and, praise the Lord, it wasn't Mike. The rest of the trip was slow, but uneventful. Mike had a great weekend and thought I had gone away, not to college, but to a resort called Lafayette.

Right after Rush Week at the end of January, a vote for a new slate of fraternity officers was taken. The term included the second semester of your junior year and the first semester of your senior year. This was the year when our class would rule, and I ran for president of the fraternity.

This was not my idea, but rather suggested by someone whose name is lost to history. With this off-handed suggestion, my ego soared and the gears started to turn in the back of my head. No one likes to lose, so the first thing I did was to size up the competition. Ed Ahart was definitely running and there may have been others, but I can't recall. This wasn't going to be "Rick Moore by acclimation," but rather a horse race.

I clearly wanted to be elected but didn't really know how to campaign without looking like a jerk. So I did nothing, figuring that the brothers knew us well enough to make a decision. After all, this was a popularity contest without anything that resembled a platform. Actually, I was uncomfortable asking for votes or, said another way, I was not a good politician.

A few folks who wanted me to be elected told me that our class was solid for me, but the sophomores and seniors were split between Ed and me. I also heard, but could not confirm, that Ed was half-jokingly telling people that if I was elected and needed to represent the fraternity in front of the Dean, I would likely be drunk or hung over. All's fair in war, and there was some truth to this claim. At first, I actually thought this would gain me votes. Upon reflection, I concluded that I needed to do a little campaigning on my own. So, in the few days before the vote (don't peak too early), I talked to several seniors who I thought were on the fence. It worked and I won, by how much I will never know. It doesn't matter. I became president and Ed vice president. I called Mom and told her the news, trying to be cool about it, but bursting with pride.

Part of my pride, was the fact that my father had been president of his fraternity in high school, having not made it to college. It was custom in his day to present the president with the 'gavel' he had used to preside over meetings. It was a beautiful remembrance of his service and Mom gave it to me when he died. So at the end of my term, I kept the gavel I had used and started a new Chi Phi tradition. If my house were to catch on fire, the gavels would be the first things I would take while running to safety.

As it turned out, we never had a run-in with the Dean and being president wasn't a heavy lift. Most of the hard work was done by the social chairman, pledge master, and those in charge of the kitchen. I just presided. One huge benefit was that the president got the best suite in the house his senior year. This was largely because it was the only suite with a phone. It's hard today to imagine this good fortune. You could make a phone call anytime, without 30 brothers hearing every word.

Unlike today's Chi Phi fraternity, where there is close contact with the national organization and many active alumni, me included, we had little in the 1960s. Bruce Drinkhouse, who was in his 40s, lived on the Hill and was our contact with the adult world. He was not what you would call a forceful personality, and we never were quite sure what he did. As president, I knew he collected the money and paid the bills, but not much more. That should tell you something. Watching the money was of course important, but we didn't think so at the time. We saw him maybe twice a year. Things ran pretty much the same every year and we got all the other routine stuff done.

We had a faculty advisor from time to time, but it wasn't a particular close relationship. At one point we befriended a Major on the ROTC faculty. He was single and liked his Wild Turkey. He didn't have too many rules for us, and we liked that. He would take a few of us to dinner every so often and hang around on party weekends. At dinner we would be half in the bag from the Wild Turkey. If we had gotten in trouble, he had our backs. All in all, a good deal. For me it showed a side of the military that wasn't all spit and polish. I liked that too. In hindsight, he was likely gay, but it didn't occur to me at the time and wouldn't have mattered.

We also had almost no contact with the national chapter. I don't ever remember meeting anyone from national headquarters in Atlanta. Chi Phi had many more southern chapters than northern ones. Lehigh, Bucknell, Cornell, Stevens Institute, MIT, and Rutgers are the northern ones I can remember. I never went to any of these either.

A few words about a fraternity's secrets. Fraternities have all kinds of rituals and in our case, they were contained in a little black book. We weren't big into this stuff, so we eliminated most of it and developed Cliff's Notes for the rest. All the secret stuff was done in the 'Chapter' room on the third floor, essentially the attic. It was large, but had no windows and you needed to wear a black robe to participate. We had normal meetings every month or so to conduct business. I kept them short and to the point. No singing or chanting. The biggest event was the induction ceremony for new brothers, a week or so after Hell Night.

There was a long induction process similar to a church service that was included in the little black book. To go through the whole thing, for one brother, would have taken 30-40 minutes. We cut it down to five minutes. It could get hot and stuffy in the attic with robes on.

There were also secret handshakes and other crazy stuff that everyone was to learn. We never did any of it. For example, one Friday night before a football weekend with Bucknell, a few of us were in the Young Republican's (YR) Club and there were guys from Bucknell who had made the trip for the game. We got to talking at the bar and found out some were in Chi Phi. Immediately, they attempted to seal our bond with the "secret handshake." I remember saying, "What the fuck is this?"

Turns out the handshake is rather creepy. I wouldn't use it on a bet. After some confusion, we convinced them we were really Chi Phi guys by inviting them to the Rock Room. The night ended well. But back to the YR and why we were there. Pennsylvania had 'blue laws' in the 1960's that prohibited selling liquor on Sundays, unless you were a private club. The YR was a private club with a long history with Chi Phi. We all joined so on Sunday mornings we could go for brunch and have a Bloody Mary to cure our hangovers. It was such a good experience I remain a Republican to this day. Although lately, I have been embarrassed by the Party.

Being in a fraternity was not about the secret shit. It was about your bond with other guys, who you knew would look out for you in a tough spot and you would do the same for them. It also meant telling each other the truth, even if it wasn't pleasant, and respecting each other. In short, it was about growing up.

There was one time that I did exercise the power of the presidency. Phil, for a reason I can't recall, was interested in being a social member at Chi Phi our senior year rather than continue with Phi Gamma Delta. I encouraged this, but it had never been done before to anyone's knowledge. He knew a lot of us, but not so much the younger brothers. It had nothing to do with Phil, they just didn't know him. It required a vote and when the younger guys starting to ask questions, I shut them down and took a quick vote by show of hands. No one wanted to antagonize me, so he was accepted by acclamation. It worked out well.

During the periods I was not dating Alayne, I did date others. I had my share of blind dates and one I actually dated several times. She happened to be around when pictures were taken for our yearbook, so she and I are in two pictures. We had some good times, but although she was a good sport and could drink with the best of us, my drinking got the best of her too and as I recall she stopped returning my calls.

This came to a head late one Saturday night of a party weekend when we were hitching a ride with someone to her motel. We were all feeling no pain and as I was getting into the car, the call came to play another game of Wales Tales. For some unknown reason, I said yes, kissed her, and said I would see her in the morning. She drove off in a car full of people and I headed to the Rock Room. I passed out in someone's bed on the third floor and she woke me Sunday morning. You can see why she stopped answering my calls.

For another party weekend, I had no immediate prospects of a date, so I took a chance and called Lynn Mondshein from high school. Much to my surprise she accepted my invitation. I clearly would have tried earlier, but I never thought she would accept. She was likely more interested in seeing what a Lafayette weekend was like and meeting my friends, but for whatever reason she was coming.

Now my MO was for my date to arrive on Saturday afternoon for the game, or whatever else was going on. That allowed me to spend quality time in the Rock Room on Friday night (maybe Thursday too) and sleep it off Saturday morning. It also avoided the complications of sleeping arrangements for two nights. You only needed to figure out Saturday night. The standard was to get a motel room and depending on how lucky you were, you either slept in the motel or your room.

I was trying to figure out how to avoid paying for a motel room. Phil was now a social member of Chi Phi and we were close. He had an apartment downtown he shared with a friend, who I also knew. I found out that both he and his roommate were going to be out of town for the weekend so I asked if Lynn could use the apartment. Now this was a bad idea under any circumstances, but it got worse, much worse.

Lynn had every expectation of suitable accommodations and was none too happy to find out she was staying in Phil's apartment. Late Saturday night as we are about to head for the apartment, Phil informed me that both he and his roommate didn't leave, but not to worry. Lynn can sleep on the couch and I should be able to fit too. Well you can imagine where I slept that night. The next morning when I went back to pick up Lynn, she had already left. Can't blame her, I was a total jerk for saving a few bucks. More lessons learned.

I rarely left campus because you didn't need to (remember the Rock Room), and I didn't have a car until second semester senior year. There were two times I did leave, both to F&M in Lancaster, PA, about two hours away. The first time was to see the Everly Brothers in concert my sophomore year. It was in their Field House and we had bleacher type seats along the wall. I don't remember who I went with or much about the concert, but it must have been good, given the Everly Brothers. At intermission, I went to the head and on the way back bumped into Pete Brubaker, Henry's brother. He must have been on leave from the Air Force. We had a short talk and agreed to meet afterword, but never re-connected.

The second trip was impulsive my senior year. On a Friday afternoon about 3 pm we were drinking beer in preparation for a Saturday football game and party weekend. Someone said we should go to F&M because they were having some big event and had a Chi Phi chapter, where we could sleep. We could come back Saturday morning and still make all the party weekend events. At first we agreed this was a bad idea, but after a few beers, four of us climbed into Don Prough's car and headed south, Don, Shenny, Phil, and me.

After a short stop at Albright College, where we unlawfully wandered through a girls' dorm unsuccessfully looking for dates, we arrived at F&M. It was dark, the Chi Phi house was almost empty, and there was no beer on tap. It was clear we had bad intelligence about some big event. We went out, got some beer, and hoped things would get more exciting as the evening progressed. Unfortunately this did not happen and we got progressively more bored, fueled by the beer.

How my trip to the college quadrangle started, I'm not sure, but there I was in the wee hours of the morning on the Quad with a saw in my hand and lots of trees around. Someone egged me on, and I began to cut one down. It wasn't a big tree, but right on the Quad. As it started to fall, I yelled "timber" and lights started to come on in the adjacent buildings. I ran like hell and shortly found a large hedge in one corner of the campus. Thinking I was being chased to be tarred and feathered, I dove into the hedge to hide and escape. It was a cool fall night, so I burrowed under some leaves and passed out. I woke several hours later and wandered back to the Chi Phi house, slept a few more hours, and we left.

The guys got me up early so we could leave before anyone asked questions about the tree. Not my finest hour. On the way back my farts were so bad, that we stopped in a rest area and I was forced to go to the head and see if I could remedy the problem. Didn't work, but we were all so tired that we fell asleep. Unfortunately, on Route 22, Don also fell asleep. Rt. 22 was a four-lane divided highway and we were going 50-60 mph. Fortunately, the car drifted to the guard rail, glanced off, woke Don, and he gained control before we were all toast. Another bullet dodged. Back at college, the rest of the weekend seemed dull by comparison. Haven't been back to F&M since.

Now that I was officially accepted by the Army, things got a bit more serious. We had classes two or three times a week and outdoor drills on Monday from 3 to 5 pm. The class work was about Army organization with information about the "combat arms" (infantry, armor, and artillery). It was boring with much memorization, so I cut and slept through many classes. So many that one Major, not our fraternity buddy, threatened to throw me out of the program. That got my attention, so I started to attend classes, but I never paid much attention. One especially big pain in the ass was the requirement to wear your uniform to class and drill. That sucked not only because you were forever changing clothes, but I was getting fat due to a lack of exercise and a love of beer and pizza. In short, I couldn't button my uniform jacket.

One piece of good news was Carl Freemen's role in ROTC. His father was a LT Colonel in the Army and Carl was on a full ROTC scholarship. He took this stuff very seriously and as a result was the highest ranking student in our brigade. The officers let the students run a lot of the organizational stuff, so Carl gave all his fraternity brothers high ranks. Because of my poor performance, he did the best he could without the faculty asking too many questions. Carl was a wise man, stayed in the Army and retired a Major General.

In ROTC I was a captain and Carl was the colonel. This was OK with me because a captain's rank was represented by three silver circles on each shoulder of your uniform. A colonel was three silver diamonds on each shoulder. Since no one knew anything about these symbols, especially the girls, three of anything looked good and I was happy. If I had gotten promoted from a captain to a major, I would have gone from three circles to one diamond. In my mind, three was always better than one.

During junior year I spent a lot of time with Skip, Tom, and Dennis. We were all in the engineering program and Skip was my roommate. Tom and I were in civil engineering, Dennis in mechanical engineering and Skip in industrial engineering. As mentioned, we continued to play bridge almost every night in the Hogg Hall coffee shop right across from our dorm. We got along well, and I liked them very much. Skip and Dennis had serious girlfriends, whom they both eventually married. They also were not the wild type and were not frequent visitors to the Rock Room. On party weekends they each were a "couple." Dennis and Kathy were more likely to be seen having a wild time, but not so Skip and Sue.

In fact, we teased Skip, likely too much, about Sue's strait-laced ways. The big target was her hair. I don't know the style, but it was like a Barbie Doll and looked the same all the time, not a hair out of place. It was too perfect, and we just couldn't let it pass. Of course the worst thing you could say to Skip was that he was "pussy whipped" and Sue led him around by his nose. I said this too often and it did damage to our relationship. I should have known better.

Tom was also pretty strait-laced but wanted to be one of the boys. You got the impression that he was a nerd in high school as he was awkward socially. But he gave it his best shot and had a great sense of humor and laugh. He laughed at my jokes and clearly helped me more with our civil engineering homework than I helped him. I was terribly fond of Tom.

He did hit it off with one blind date, who was quite attractive. We didn't think it would last, but Tom married Ann Marie and good for him. Good for both of them! Because Skip, Tom, and Dennis were mostly otherwise occupied on party weekends, I looked for others to drink the night away.

There were more than a few nights that I passed out somewhere, not in my bed. One night a few sophomore football players from Phi Gam came over to check out the Rock Room. This was not typical, but we waved them in. We were already playing Whales Tails and they happily joined in after we explained the rules. Of course, we took advantage of their inexperience, and pretty soon everyone was in the cups.

The biggest guy, from the coal fields of western PA, turned out to be a lot of fun and when he realized that I was the president, he couldn't believe it. Why was the president getting shitfaced with the rest of the guys? He liked that idea and took a shine to me. We left the Rock Room as a gang of six or eight guys and "dropped in" at several other fraternities to drink their beer. I suggested at one point that this might piss off some people. He assured me not to worry and that I would be protected. He was about 6' 6" and 250 lbs., and indeed was correct.

After this carousing, we found our way back in the Rock Room. Barely able to stand, someone said something out of line and the beer started to fly. Unfortunately, there were other things in the Rock Room that could be put to flight. My new friend picked up a sawhorse with a blinking light that the highway department uses on construction sites and sent it sailing my way. I threw something back and this started a free-for-all that could have gotten someone hurt. Fortunately, we were so drunk the energy was just not there to cause severe damage and things shortly quieted down.

I eventually passed out in the living room and woke up the next morning with blood-stained clothes stuck to my body. Because of the IF weekend disaster previously described, I knew what to do and quickly took a shower to soften the blood and get new clothes. A bit later my new friend from Phi Gam came calling to profusely apologize. I think he liked me and the apology was genuine, but he surely didn't want a president of another fraternity pissed off at him. He was pleased I thought it all good fun, suggested we do it again, and I gained a mighty friend and protector for my remaining time at college.

This was all going on in the fall of 1967 and the spring of 1968, an eventful time in the country. Except for the war, we didn't, at least I didn't, pay much attention to the national/international news. That is until Martin Luther King, and then Bobby Kennedy, were shot. It did feel a bit like the wheels were falling off, but we were wrapped up in our own little world and generally didn't get involved in the politics. Certainly some did at Lafayette, but not the guys I hung around with. Our attention spans were quite short.

Those of us in ROTC figured we might go to Vietnam, but honestly didn't give it much thought. At that age you don't believe you will ever die (we had suppressed the memory of Arv and Gikas), and perhaps thought that the war would be over before we had to go.

18.

SUMMER OF 1968, INDIAN TOWN GAP AND FLORIDA

IF YOU WERE IN ROTC, there was a requirement to spend six weeks of basic training for future officers at Indian Town Gap near Harrisburg, PA. You could do this after either your junior or senior year. Most, including me, elected to get it over with after our junior year. Because it was six weeks, there was time before and after. I started early in July and ended two weeks before school started. The time before was spent helping Phil and Ellen at the gas station. I would have gone back to Phil after summer camp, but Alton Roberts was taking a vacation to Florida and needed some company, so he asked me to go.

Now Alton was five years older and a Lutheran minister, who I had known since I was a kid. He grew up in Cresskill and did some of his training for the ministry at the church we both went to. He was a terrific guy and a very progressive minister, nevertheless he was a MINISTER. I hesitated a moment because of this, but it was such a great opportunity to get away and he was a good guy, so I said yes. Then I found out we would be driving his GTO convertible with a stereo tape deck. Good decision. More on that trip later. First, summer camp.

Indian Town Gap consisted of a large number of old wooden buildings from WWII on a huge flat plateau that faded into foothills in central Pennsylvania, about 30 minutes north of Harrisburg. You could see a gap in the hills off to the west, which apparently gave this

God-forsaken place its name. There were six-week sessions starting at different times over the summer. As mentioned, ours started early in July. Each session was organized around a battalion, with 4 companies. Each company in turn had four platoons. The platoon was the basic unit of about 40 guys, who all slept in one of the many two-story wooden barracks. There were about 500 guys in the battalion.

There were bunk beds and one shower room on each floor of the barracks. Each platoon had an officer and non-commissioned officer (NCO) as an advisor. Our officer was a major and he slept in an apartment on the other side of the post. The NCO, a master sergeant, slept in a small room at one end of the first floor. Opposite the Sargent's bedroom was an office that was used by the Major and "Sarg" to conduct the business associated with our training, including facts and figures on our individual performances.

We came from all over the east coast from many colleges and universities. It was fun to get to know each other and size up the "competition." Yes, you were to be graded on everything you did, with the information sent back to Lafayette to be used in organizing our senior year. It became very clear who was serious about getting good "grades" and who was not. Guess what group I fell into?

I was very smug, considering I was the president of a fraternity. What else could the Army teach me about leadership? I was wrong, again, but this was only partly about leadership. It was mostly about the nuts and bolts of how the Army works. I, along with most others, couldn't have cared less. This was NOT a volunteer Army, we were just doing our two years and would figure things out when we got our first assignment in the real Army. Playing games in the dust of Indian Town Gap didn't fire up our competitive juices.

I quickly bonded with a few like-minded trainees, one from Norwich, in Vermont, and one from the University of Virginia, as I remember. We, and a few others, formed the "resistance" in our platoon, while there were many in the middle who just wanted to keep their heads down and finish. The last group, on the other end of the spectrum, were trying hard to be excellent soldiers. One guy was from

West Point, why I never found out. He was clearly in the last group.

We believed that there needed to be some humor, fresh air, and common sense injected into the Army to keep it from going rogue and overthrowing the government. We were representing "the people" in an otherwise internally focused organization and we were there to keep an eye on things. Remember this was 1968 and there was much distrust of institutions throughout the country. We were the "good guys" on the inside. We felt the country would be pleased to know that we were watching out for its interest and the Constitution.

Like many organizations that require obedience and fidelity to a chain of command, there was a system of demerits if you did something wrong. Our group of resisters quickly concluded that a measure of our commitment would be the number of demerits awarded by Sarg. You got them for a sloppy bed, poorly shined boots, an unclean weapon, or just doing dumb things.

One of the three of us were always in the lead, which changed often. We laughed about it, which kept our stress levels down. I had no trouble getting demerits because I hadn't paid attention in ROTC class back at Lafayette, so had no clue about all the Army bullshit. This became painfully apparent in the first week.

Every day you had some kind of training, usually a combination of field and classroom work. After breakfast the company was organized to march or run to a classroom or field exercise. Actually, running in the Army is called the airborne scuffle, which is a slow run that is often done to the rhythm of chants. The chants are fun and help you ignore the pain of long marches. For example:

Me and Superman had a fight
I hit him with a left and I hit him with a right
Hit him so hard nearly busted his brain
Now I'm datin' Lois lane

At breakfast you found out who among you were to be the company commander and platoon leaders for the day. On the first

Wednesday, I drew the short straw and was assigned as company commander.

This meant that I was to march/airborne scuffle the entire company to our assigned training location. It included four platoons, or about 120 guys. Now, the whole purpose of our Monday afternoon drills at Lafayette was to perfect our marching skills, based on all the good classroom instruction I had slept through. Things were looking bleak that Wednesday morning as I took command of the company with 120 guys in formation looking at me for instructions.

I knew they needed to turn right (right face!) and start walking (marching!), but that required about five individual commands, none of which I knew. Things like attention, port arms (everyone had a rifle), right face, forward march, all given in the correct order. It became apparent very quickly that I had no idea what to do. Sarg stepped in (one demerit) and helped get the gang going.

Now the hard part, accelerating into the airborne scuffle and stopping. With a little more help from Sarg (another demerit), we got into the airborne scuffle and we actually sang several chants to put us all in good spirits. The problem was stopping. I didn't know how. I yelled something that I thought sounded good, like: "slow down, you fucking idiots." At first, I thought this actually worked as the first two platoons slowed down. The problem was that the second platoon didn't stop and ran into the first. You could hear the rifles bang against each other as everyone tried to keep their balance. A colossal fuck-up (two more demerits).

After 30 to 45 minutes of total chaos, we reached our morning training session: the care and use of the M-60 machine gun. We were to have classroom training first and then shoot in the afternoon. The training was outside on large tables and, as we all sat down, I tried to hide from the instructor, another major. Unfortunately, Sarg had apparently told him of my poor marching performance and so he started to pick on me with several questions that I was supposed to know, but of course didn't. More humiliation. After some time, the instructor lost interest and I hung my head for the rest of the morning.

In the afternoon we first had to take apart and put back together the M-60 to familiarize ourselves with the machine gun, up close and personal. Bullets are expensive and they didn't want us to have too much time for live fire. So we trained and trained, including breaking the gun down and putting it back together blindfolded. Right before the live fire, we had a contest to see how fast we could break down and put the gun back together -- no blind folds this time.

We were in groups of four, so we had to pick the fastest guy to compete with the rest of the groups. I was picked. There must have been 25-30 groups, each with their best guy ready to perform. I rose to the occasion and everyone in my group said I won, if only by a second or so. Naturally, Sarg and the Major weren't going to let me win, after my morning performance, so they picked another group. I felt I let my group down, but they were good sports as they yelled that a miscarriage of justice had occurred.

Sarg knew what happened, but he did it because he didn't like my attitude one bit. He was bound to make me and my buddies pay for our cockiness, but he did respect my speed with the M-60.

When we finally got back to our barracks after one of the longest days of my life, our Major, who wasn't with us most of the day, summoned me to the little office on the first floor. He was in the infantry, so marching was a big deal to him and I'm sure he thought I was being disrespectful. He was very stern and said I needed to shape up or I would be ranked last in the platoon. To start my recovery, he gave me his copy of FM-22-5, the Army Field Manual for Close Order Drill. I said thank you, left, and never opened good old FM-22-5. I figured I wouldn't be CO again and therefore wouldn't need to study. Fortunately, I was right on that one. God bless the infantry, but it wasn't for me.

So "Machine Gun Wednesday" was over. On Thursday, Friday, and Saturday, we had our training with rifles. Thursday was all classroom stuff and we focused on the M-16, which was the standard rifle in the Army at the time, and I think still is, slightly modified. You could fire the M-16 either automatic or semiautomatic with a clip of 20 rounds.

We were taught only to put 18 rounds in the clip, because 20 could jam the spring mechanism. We were also told to fire the weapon only on semiautomatic, where you could shoot as fast as you could pull the trigger: one pull = one bullet. Firing automatic, where you held the trigger down and the bullets kept coming, was not recommended. It's more difficult to control automatic fire, as the bullets spray all over the place.

If the North Vietnamese Army (the bad guys) are charging you en masse, you can actually kill more of the bastards on semiautomatic as you pick individual bodies off one at a time, 18 in total if you start with a full clip and if you can keep your cool. If you switch to automatic and depress the trigger, the 18 rounds will be gone so quickly you will never get 18 KIAs. Fun facts.

The M-16 is more effective at close range in the jungle but needs to be well taken care of and cleaned often, or it will jam. When the Marines initially went to Vietnam, they were prone to drag the M-16 through the mud. Not a good idea, as they found out.

Another thing they told you was that as an officer you don't need to carry a rifle. Sounds strange, but your main job in a firefight is to coordinate action and call for help (other troops, mortars, artillery, and air support, either helicopters or jets). This keeps you way too busy to be shooting. If things get bad enough so you need to shoot, there will be plenty of rifles lying around left by the dead soldiers.

On Friday and Saturday, we went to the firing range, but we had to use the older M-14s and not the M-16s, which were all in use in SE Asia. The two rifles are very different. The M-14 is only semiautomatic and fires a larger 30-caliber bullet at a slower velocity. It's heavier than the M-16, but easier to shoot and more accurate at distance. The M-16 fires the smaller 7.26 mm NATO around at a higher velocity and is better to kill people at close range, but it's harder to fire accurately at distance, especially on automatic.

The slower M-14 bullet spins in the air and when it hits a body, is more likely to make a small entry hole, go right through, and exit the same way. The M-16 round goes in the same way (small hole), but its higher velocity makes it unstable, so it begins to tumble, ripping up everything inside and making a huge exit wound. A deadly human killing machine. A good reason they should be banned from domestic use.

So back to the rifle range. There was plenty of M-14 ammo, so we had plenty of time to shoot on Friday. The targets were 100 yards away and huge, 6 feet by 6 feet. The bull's eye was about 8 inches across. We had to practice in four positions: prone, sitting, kneeling, and standing. Each were progressively more difficult, but to help, you could disconnect the sling from the butt end of the rifle, wrap it around your upper left arm, and use it to steady the rifle. This was especially helpful in the prone and sitting positions where your left arm became a tripod with your elbow as the contact point, resting either on the ground (prone position) or your knee (sitting position).

With my freshman ROTC rifle team training, I did quite well and on Friday spent most of the afternoon helping guys who couldn't hit the side of a barn. About 1/3 of us had never fired a weapon of any kind.

Friday was practice. Saturday was the day to test your marksmanship and qualify with the rifle.

Friday evening our Major announced that he would buy beer at the bar next to the PX for anyone who qualified as an expert marksman on Saturday. Saturday night was to be the first time we were allowed in the bar. Unbeknownst to the Major, several of us had been to the bar every night since we had found it on the previous Tuesday. At 50 cents for a large pitcher of beer, it was hard not to drop in after a hard day in the field. After my terrible performance on Wednesday, I needed a beer, and figured if I got caught, it would cost only a few more demerits. The Major was all excited about introducing his "top guns" to the bar and telling some war stories. Further, the Major figured it couldn't possibly cost him much.

On the range during qualification you got 10 rounds to fire in each of the four positions. Depending on how well you did, you fell into one of several levels, with expert being the top level. If you didn't hit anything, and some didn't, you were in the lowest level.

Everyone got a medal, depending on your level of expertise. Enlisted troops commonly wore their medal over their left pocket, but officers rarely did. Nevertheless, as you might expect, competence with firearms was an important part of being in the Army. I established my competence by firing my first 20 rounds in the bull's eye. I thought that would have qualified me as expert, even if I completely missed the next 20, but I didn't. Given my time at the rifle range in Easton, it was rather easy.

Turns out my two buddies from Norwich and UVA also shot expert, as did the West Point guy and one other in our platoon. The two other guys didn't drink, so the three amigos were about to take some of the Major's money. When he showed up at the bar that night and found us sitting at his table, he was none too happy, but did his best to be one of the guys. As expected, he told a few stories, had a beer, and left to allow us to enjoy the rest of the night. As he was leaving, he reminded us that he was paying and that we should keep track of the bill and he would pay us back the next day.

We did indeed enjoy the evening. We got roaring drunk and got back to the barracks way after bed check. We tried to sneak in but were falling over each other and made a racket. We were hoping Sarg didn't notice, but of course he did. It was a giveaway when he woke us in the morning with all our clothes on from the night before, and our breath took the paint off the walls.

Sarg cut us some slack given that the Major "got us drunk." The next step was to collect our money. Over breakfast, we tallied the number of pitchers we had to the best of our memory and arrived at a cost of 6 bucks as I remember. That's 12 pitchers, or four each, and I think we missed a few. I was elected to collect the money because I was already in the Major's doghouse and things couldn't get much worse for me. The guys also made some weak argument that collecting the money was a way for me to get even with the Major. Believe me I wanted as little to do with the Major as possible. Nevertheless, I got the assignment.

Later that morning the Major arrived and went into his little office, a place I didn't like. I finally got the courage to enter and reminded him of his obligation. Without looking up, he said "how much?" I mumbled the 6 bucks and he stiffened in his chair. He looked up as if to say we could not have possibly consumed that much beer. There were only three of us. I confirmed the number and he paid without saying a word. I was now in the cellar of his doghouse.

After that first week things settled down to the boredom of training and more training, with fewer demerits. But according to Sarg, I could never get my boots polished or my rifle cleaned to a standard he accepted. There were, however, two other events of interest that summer at Indian Town Gap. My 21st birthday and Tactical Training of the Individual Solder (TTIS).

My birthday fell on a Saturday and it so happened we had a pass from noon that Saturday to Sunday at 6 pm. On Saturday, as soon as Sarg thought my rifle was clean enough, I headed to the front gate. Going home seemed too long a trip, so I headed toward Philly, hoping to visit one of my college friends in the area. I tried contacting a few from pay phones, but no one was around. So I hitchhiked into town. I was determined not to spend my birthday at the Gap.

I arrived around dinner time and ate in some cheap restaurant, since I didn't have much cash and no credit cards. I got a room in a rooming house, stopped in a few bars and, a bit lonely, went to bed early. The next day I took the bus to Easton and had a great Sunday dinner at the Aharts'. They made me feel like family and it made the trip worthwhile. Then I hitchhiked back to the Gap in no time along Route 22. It was a good and safe way to travel in those days.

Most of our training was designed to make us familiar with Army ways and to prepare us to be officers in the U.S. Army. But some was nitty gritty stuff that every GI had to go through in basic training. This was best illustrated in the TTIS field exercise, where you were a grunt for two days. You carried all the equipment that a GI would in combat (field pack, rifle, ammo, c-rations, canteen, shovel, etc.) and wandered through the woods.

At the end of the second day, you came to a dusty field that was about 100 yards wide with barbed wire obstacles everywhere. This was the last part of TTIS. You needed to get across the field while the instructors were firing machine guns over your head. Blanks were used, but it sure felt and sounded like live fire. The fire required you to stay low and for long stretches you had to do the low crawl under the barbed wire with your belly on the ground and your rifle cradled in your arms. Even for 10 yards this was very difficult, as you ate the dust and scraped your elbows and knees.

I finally made it through and slumped down next to a tree, exhausted. I got my canteen out for a drink, but got the brilliant idea to have a chocolate drink, since our c-rations contained a packet of chocolate powder. So I found the packet and with great excitement tore off the top and poured it into my canteen. What I didn't realize, because I didn't read the instructions, was that for the chocolate to dissolve, the water needed to be HOT.

So when I took a long swig from the canteen, all I got was the dry chocolate powder that didn't mix with the water, but did mixed with the dust already in my mouth. I gagged and choked for some time, to the point where they were about to call the medic. Once I collected my wits, I realized that the water was undrinkable and so I suffered all the way back to the barracks. Lessons learned. Among other things, read the instructions.

Finally, after a long six weeks, we left. I wasn't last in my platoon, but close. My good shooting saved the day.

There wasn't much time between my release and leaving for Florida with Alton. We drove all the way and he did most of the driving. Our first stop was in Newport News, VA, where his uncle lived. Free room and board. However, as we were riding through the Virginia countryside, Alton gave me a bit of background on his uncle and aunt. Seems their one son had committed suicide and understandably they were having trouble coming to grips and accepting this unfortunate event.

To help deal with their grief, they became interested in Edgar Casey and his belief that he could communicate with the dead, among other things. Another one of Casey's beliefs was that the world was going to end soon, by violent volcanic events and rising seas (maybe he was on to something), and that one of the few places not flooded would be the Newport News area in Virginia. Seems they had moved to this part of Virginia for this reason.

This was quite a bit to take in for a free meal and lodging, but I was game. Turns out the subject of their son, and good old Edgar, never came up, except for a passing reference by Alton when he said grace at dinner. They were very nice people and we left bright and early the next morning.

After driving for the next two days, we arrived in Miami with the top down and The Mamas & The Papas playing on the tape deck. We stayed at a motel near the Fontainebleau Hotel, on Collins Avenue. One afternoon we went to Hialeah to watch the dogs run and place a few small bets. Alton was friendly with everyone and soon we were talking to two young ladies at the track.

Turns out they were also from NJ, not too far from Alton. Since they had been dropped off by other friends, Alton kindly offered to drive them back to their motel, which was remarkably close to ours.

They were pleased to find their ride was a GTO convertible, with the ever-ready tape deck. As we were driving down Collins Avenue with the top down and the music playing, the young lady sitting in the front seat next to Alton asked what he did for a living. When he said a Lutheran minister, they both laughed and thought it was the best pick-up line they had heard in quite a while.

This prompted much discussion and finally Alton invited them to attend a Sunday service and see for themselves. Later we met their friends, had dinner and some laughs, but that was that. They went on their way, and we went ours the next day.

Next stop was Naples on the west coast. One of Mother's friends won a promotion to stay two free nights at a motel near Lehigh Acres and gave it to us. The catch was we needed to hear their pitch to sell lots in what was the start of the building boom on Florida's west coast. Alton had no interest and I had no money, so we ate their breakfast, heard their pitch, saw the planned subdivision, and left. Would have been a great investment, if I had had two nickels to rub together.

That night we found a fish buffet and had many, many shrimp. We lingered awhile, because they had a TV in the dining room and the 1968 Republican Convention was on and about to nominate Richard Nixon for president. I was politically illiterate and thought the convention rather boring, but got a terrific civic lesson from Alton on how the system worked.

Then we were off for our last stop, with a college friend of Alton living in the Orlando area. They lived near a lake and I got my first chance to water-ski. Did rather well for my first try and zipped around the lake a few times. Alton's friend was married and we stayed with them at their townhouse. They were both Egyptian and I got the impression that at least one of the families had some money.

There was a lot of discussion about the Middle East and the recent 6-day war. Alton was an anti-Zionist, thinking that an Israeli State in the middle of millions of Arabs was a bad idea. I just listened, as I knew almost nothing about conditions in the Middle East. Again, like American politics, I got an education by listening to Alton and his friends. I still agree with them.

But, truth be told, the best part of the conversation was being with his friend's wife. Not only was she a wonderful person and very bright (I think she was getting a master's or Ph.D.) and a good cook, but she was one of the most beautiful women I had ever seen. Classic Egyptian beauty.

The trip over, we headed north for my senior year. We didn't come back empty-handed, however. On the last day, I bought a small palm tree, about 4 feet high with the dirt bulb in a bucket. We put it in the back seat (Alton was a good sport), and off we drove north.

19.

SENIOR YEAR

WITH GOOD CLASSES SENIOR year, that I actually took an interest in, getting decent grades wasn't going to be a big lift. This combined with being president of the fraternity was the recipe for a great year. And in fact, it was.

As I mentioned, the civil engineering program was heavily weighted toward structural engineering. However, we had a new faculty member who was young and taught one class in environmental engineering. It focused on water, wastewater, and environmental pollution in general. I liked the course, in part because it was different than structures, but don't remember thinking this would turn out to be my lifelong professional interest.

This is illustrated by the fact that I had job interviews mostly with structural/construction firms. We were blessed by having firms come to campus to interview us, since the job market/economy was strong. I got lucky, again, and landed a job with Chicago, Bridge and Iron (CBI) along with another CE friend, Dick Sherry. Their home office wasn't in Chicago and they didn't build bridges or work with iron, but otherwise a great company, which is still around.

Likely the best part of senior year was living in the fraternity house and not the dorm. This was like the difference between a Motel 6 and the Ritz. Not only did I live in the house, but as president I got the best room with the only phone, other than the one on the first floor. Skip and I shared one of the six suites on the second floor. We each had a bedroom off a central living room where the phone was located. I had died and gone to heaven.

The first thing I did was place my palm tree in the living area at the end of the couch. A chair, end table, and coffee table finished the room. Other than the palm tree, I can't remember where we got the furniture, which might have come from Good Will. We each also had a bed, dresser, desk, and bookcase in the bedroom, which were owned by the fraternity. We kept things pretty tidy and loved the arrangement.

My biggest responsibility was watering the palm tree. Since this palm tree took in water through its leaves, you couldn't just add water to the pot it was planted in. So, when I took a shower, I would take the tree along and pretend it was raining. This worked fine until Thanksgiving vacation. It was never the same vibrant green after that, and it died over Christmas break. A great run and conversation piece while it lasted.

I wasn't dating Alayne most of first semester, so I was free and easy. If I had any fantastic dates, they have faded from memory. Also the trips to the Rock Room began to blur together. One night we were feeling no pain and a few of us wandered into our suite. It was likely that Skip and Sue were in his room with the door locked and we wanted to give them some good-natured shit. Peter McCue was there and for some reason we became engaged in some form of physical contact. I think it was instigated by Emil Sommer. As we spun around, we fell on the couch and our combined weight (>400 lbs.) snapped all four legs.

From that point on, the couch was on the floor without the legs. At first we thought this would be a problem. Oh contraire. This became another conversation piece and served two important purposes. First, by essentially sitting on the floor, you got a much better view of the palm tree, looking up. Second and perhaps more important, once you got your date on the floor, I mean couch, and pointed out the lovely palm tree, you were all set to take things to the next level.

As usual, parents' weekend had a football game and afterward everyone came back to the house for a cocktail party. Mom came to all the parents' weekends and this was no exception. As an added treat, Leslie came too. I can't remember why. Perhaps to help Mother with the driving, but more likely to check out the scene of her terrible blind date, now that her little brother ran the place. For that reason and because she was visibly pregnant, she was treated like royalty and loved it.

Everyone was well-behaved and standing around in small groups talking and drinking at the cocktail party. We were in the foyer and the front door was open. All of a sudden we heard a "crack," like a bowling ball hitting granite. One of the juniors, a big guy, had too much to drink, passed out, keeled over backward, and hit his head on the granite doorsill.

I was about 10 feet away and by the sound of things and the way he looked, it was panic time. He had passed out and at 220 pounds, was not so easy to move. Four guys carried him up to the second floor and dumped him on a bed in the nearest room. He didn't live in the house, so it wasn't his bed. I had made sure it wasn't mine either. In the short time it took to take him upstairs, he must have lost 10 pounds in sweat. He was soaking wet, as were his clothes. Once on the bed, he mumbled something, so we left him to dry out and sober up. Of course, in hindsight, we should have called an ambulance and were lucky it wasn't much worse. As I recall, he was dancing at the party later that night. Dodged a bullet and another bad story about too much drinking at fraternities!

Speaking of drinking, we did our fair share, and I was lucky I didn't pay more serious consequences, other than bad hangovers. After most football games and cocktail parties, we would all go to the same restaurant downtown for dinner, a fraternity tradition. It wasn't fancy and had a very short menu. There was steak and a few other things, but everyone had steak. To get to the place you went to the circle in downtown Easton and took Main Street west. Main street was wide with many cross streets as you were driving uphill. There were several traffic lights where the street flattened out going through the inter-section. One time we were coming back in Bob Rufe's car. He had continued to drink with great gusto during dinner and neglected to stop at any of the traffic lights as we returned down Main Street. He was traveling rather fast and at every intersection with a signal, where the road flattened out, we bounced through, no matter what color the light. Everyone was laughing, but something deep in my brain was sending signals of distress. By the time I got my wits together, we were at the circle and safe.

Once back at the House, there was some down time to change clothes and wait until the band started playing, typically from 9 to midnight. Everything was moved out of the foyer, including the rug. The band set up at the dining room end of the foyer and we danced on the hardwood floor. Most of the beer stayed in the Rock Room, but some always made it to the dance floor. There was another tradition that was prompted when the floor got slippery with beer. You cleared a path, took a few quick steps and belly flopped on the floor, sliding across the room. This was crazy and you needed to be well-lubricated, because it was hard on the body. I did it once and of course ruined my shirt in the process. Maybe my pants too. Needless to say, dates didn't like this, at least the good ones.

Dates did like to dance, and the music of the late 60's was a magical time to dance. That's for both fast and slow music (Four Seasons, Temptations, Marvin Gaye, Elvis, Aretha Franklin, Righteous Brothers, Beach Boys, Wilson Pickett, to say nothing of the Beatles and many more). The recent success of the Broadway musical Jersey Boys (about the Four Seasons), is a testament to the enduring appeal of this music. It's really terrific entertainment, I recommend.

I really got into fast dancing because the beats were so easy to follow. You could dance together or apart and switch back and forth through the song. The exercise also help keep you sober. Slow dancing, well what can I say, it was beautiful. You didn't just stand and squeeze a sweaty body, you needed to dance to what were also wonderful beats. All in all I learned to love to dance, but only with a partner who had some rhythm.

Since Dad died, Mother and I spent Christmas with Leslie and Henry. This year was again in Vermont, as Henry was teaching political science at the University of Vermont. Vermont was beautiful at Christmas and even in the 60s, Burlington was a lovely small town, which hadn't yet discovered its waterfront. That happened later when the old piers and warehouses gave way to restaurants and condos.

On Christmas Eve, Leslie suggested we go to a church in Underhill, VT for the traditional 11 p.m. evening service. She had heard it was worth the 30-minute ride on a cold winter night. Underhill was at the foot of the Green Mountains and in the winter, the windy road over the mountains through Smuggler's Notch was closed. It was the last stop. Henry stayed home with little Jill.

The church was huge and white and located at one end of the town green. It was picture perfect and decorated for the holidays in that understated New England way. We took a slow ride around the green to take in all the town decorations. The church was stark and white inside, and the pews were getting filled as we sat down.

The service was traditional and there was a real treat at the end. The choir was large and good, but there was a guest who had grown up in Underhill and was back for Christmas. He happened to be a professional opera singer and at the end of the service stood and sang O Holy Night. It had to be the most moving piece of music I have ever heard. In part we weren't expecting it and in part it would have been amazing anywhere. To hear it in little Underhill, at the end of the road, was completely special. I had tears in my eyes.

As an added treat, it had started snowing during the service and as we left, the snow had lightly covered the Green. Talk about a Currier & Ives picture. I don't think we said anything the whole ride back, contemplating what had just happened.

Back at school, I entered the final semester which turned into a victory lap. It was made better since at some point Alayne and I got back together in about as serious a way as I was capable of at the time. My lack of seriousness was illustrated the weekend of the ROTC Ball. This was one of the traditional party weekends in the spring semester when there were no football games. It occurred in late February.

For some reason Alayne couldn't make the weekend, so I was going to get dressed in my uniform and go alone. No problem. The Friday night before the Saturday dance, a few of us were at the YR (Young Republican's Club previously mentioned) having a beer or two. Carl and I picked up two local young ladies and decided to go to Jack's to end the night.

At this point I had the VW Beetle that was my graduation present from Mom. A sweet little blue job, great downhill and not so good uphill. The four of us climbed in the Beetle and headed for Jack's. Going up college hill took forever, especially with four people in the car. We were in good humor chatting away, and I wasn't paying proper attention with the peddle to the floor. When we reached the top of the hill, I neglected to take my foot off the gas and we picked up speed as we hit the curve in front of the ROTC building.

I realized too late that we were going too fast and, try as I might, we didn't quite make the turn. The back right wheel hit the curb and after bouncing off, we came to a stop. Fortunately, there were no other cars on the road, and no one was hurt. But the back axle had been bent and when I drove away, the whole car wobbled. This was clearly a problem, but we were not to be deterred. We wobbled back to the house, a short ride across campus, parked the car, and climbed into Carl's car to complete our trip to Jack's.

The next morning, I was hungover in the worst sort of way, but pulled myself out of bed and tried to fix the car. I tried my best, but you just can't straighten a bent axle by hand, or any other way for that matter. After an hour or so I gave up and lumbered back into the house where I ran into Carl. He reminded me that I had asked the young lady I was with to the ROTC dance. I was sick, didn't have a car, and was depressed because I didn't have the money to get it fixed. I told him I would have to call it off, but didn't have her last name or phone number.

I went back to bed and the phone woke me late afternoon. Someone came in to tell me there was a girl asking for me. I told her I was sick and couldn't make it. At least I sounded like I was sick, but I felt like a real heel, because I was. So much for being a Master of the Universe.

A word about Jack's. Jack was born in 1900, which I thought was pretty cool, and something I could easily remember. He was, by his own admission, a vaudeville performer in his younger days, although what exactly he performed wasn't entirely clear. As the story goes, sometime in the early 1950s he was performing at the burlesque theater in Allentown, PA. On his day off, he happened to wander into a small bar just north of Easton, PA, less than an hour from Allentown. He took a shine to the bartender and owner, the widow Katie. One thing led to another and he spent the night. He never left.

Jack and Katie lived together, but never got married. It worked and they had a good relationship with the boys from Lafayette. There was a small u-shaped bar at one end of the main room, which also had several tables and a pool table. There was a second room which was more a dining room, a term used loosely, given the quality of Katie's food.

Jack held court behind the bar and, if you were lucky, quoted Shakespeare or Kipling from his vaudeville days. Quite a show. Phil and I were not quite regulars, but Jack knew us well. One night we played pool with two guys from Lehigh. Phil was good, and even though he didn't have his cue, he played like Minnesota Fats and we took them to the cleaners. Several free drinks followed. On another occasion, Phil played a game at the bar where Jack would name a song, and someone needed to name the singer. Phil had an encyclopedic memory of this stuff and dominated the game. Again, more free drinks. Hands down, my fondest memory was Jack quoting Gunga Din, while standing behind the bar late at night. Amazing! Laurence Olivier couldn't have done it better.

The spring IF (interfraternity) weekend was one that Alayne could make. This was the one where we rented a place in the Poconos for a good price, since it was before the summer season. As a senior you got one of the best rooms, in this case one of the little cottages. We took a page from Skip and Sue and spent a good deal of the weekend in the cottage with the door locked.

There has been much written about the 'free love' movement in the late 1960's, that went along with civil rights, war protesting, hippies and Woodstock. Again, like I previously mentioned, we were in our isolated bubble on campus and like many seismic cultural changes, didn't fully appreciate what we were going through. Surely, 20 year old guys have always had sky high testosterone and sexual conquests were a badge of honor. We were no different and perhaps the new norms allowed the girls to be a bit freer. This last part is pure speculation on my part, because I never had discussions with my friends about specific sexual encounters. Things were done behind close doors and no one, to my knowledge, knew who took their close off and who didn't. My suspicion is that sex occurred largely between people with long term relationships, and that one night stands were rare. By my unofficial account, at least 7 of my fraternity brothers had long term college relationships that turned into marriage, and they all lasted. Congratulations!

As the weather got warm at the end of May, there was a fraternity tradition between Chi Phi and our next door neighbor, Delta Tau Delta (DTD). It was a water balloon fight. It was great fun, even though they had slightly higher ground. To make up the difference we got some surgical elastic cord and made a slingshot. There were two pieces about 10 feet long with a cloth pocket tied in the middle. Two guys would hold the ends and a third, the shooter, would load the cloth pocket with a water balloon. He would then pull back on the cords, aim, and let the balloon fly. Done wrong and the shooter got wet, but done right and you have a formidable weapon. Everyone kept their eye on the sling shot (DTD had one too) because you didn't want to get hit with a water balloon going about 60 mph. It could knock you out.

Guys from each House would attack each other and throw balloons, with little impact other than getting wet. It went on for an hour or two, with great spirit and a window or two broken by the slingshot. Everyone was always looking for an edge, so senior year someone got the brilliant idea to fill one or two balloons with grease and fat from the kitchen. This was nasty. The first one missed the target (DTD's house) and hit the road in front of their house. The second one hit the side of the house, exploded, and the shit went everywhere. We won that year, and DTD was pissed.

The really bad part was the next day, when the temperature got into the high 80s and the sun baked the grease and fat. The smell was sickening and we tried to make amends by cleaning up the mess. It was not possible, but at least the temperatures dropped as did the smell and the natural decay process took its course. Bad idea, but good story. I was glad my term as president had ended.

With the nice spring weather, Phil got the idea of taking a canoe trip down the Delaware River. Actually we took two trips. The first from Easton downriver to New Hope PA and the second from the Delaware Water Gap downriver to Easton. The first was the most interesting based on a miscalculation on our part. The geniuses that we were figured the river would be high in the Spring with a strong current. Based on a current of 3 feet per second increased to 5 feet per second with our expert paddling, we figured we could get the New Hope easily in 8 hours. We had two canoes with Phil and me in one and Shenny and Emil in the other. With a few six-packs and sandwiches, we departed Easton at 8 am. The day before we had left a car in New Hope for the ride back.

We were having a great old time yelling 'white water' every time we saw a few ripples. Then we reached one of the islands in the river. We went one way and Shenny and Emil went the other, as things were starting to get a bit competitive. We paddled feverishly and made the end of the island first. A few minutes later along came Shenny and Emil, but all you could see were their heads and shoulders. They had tipped the canoe, but somehow stayed in it and were now bouncing along the bottom totally out of control due to the force of the current. It was quite a sight, which unfortunately was not captured on film.

We came to their rescue and helped them run aground on a sand bar. They emptied the canoe, but had lost the remaining beer. We gave them a real bad time about their canoe skills and had a good laugh. Losing the beer was the least of our worries as we came to realize that we had only gone a few miles in almost two hours. The river generally widened below Easton, more 'lake like', with a much reduced current and periodic heads winds. We had badly underestimated our travel time. We paddled with great vigor for the next 10 hours and made New Hope just before dark. We slept well that night.

To balance out our nature trips we have a few road trips to NY City. We would drive in on Saturday afternoon, spent the night bar hopping and crash at Mon's in Cresskill. She helped sober us up with a good Sunday brunch. One Saturday night we were downtown around Greenwich Village and NYU. There were four of us, but we got split up as Peter McCue and I picked up two co-eds and headed to a bar. The girls suggested a place and it turned out to be a fancy night club. Live band and a standup comic at intermission. Someone said that Sammy Davis Junior was in a front row table to hear the comic. We couldn't be sure, but it looked like him. It was a great time until the check came. It was several hundred dollars and between Peter and I, we had less than $100.

Now this was panic time. After assessing our combined resources, I leaned over to Peter and said we were in deep shit. He suggested we tell the truth and ask for mercy. It was wise advice, which Peter continued to give throughout his successful professional career in public relations. So I went up to the front door and told our tale of woe to two guys who looked like they could make decisions. Sure enough, they took what money we had and actually told us to come back, providing we could pay our bill the next time. They even let us keep 5 bucks to get home. We dodged a bullet and I'm not sure the girls even realized what happened. Never saw the girls, the Club or Sammy Davis again.

A second time we were on the Upper East Side in a bar on Second Avenue. It may have been St. Patrick's Day weekend. In any event, we were there at closing at 2 am. Since we were inside we could stay a bit longer to finish our last drinks. There were four of us and as we were leaving Ren Drews and I walked down the bar and finished any glasses that were at least half full. We were feeling no pain. Outside, on the side walk, we were trying to remember where we had parked the car. At this point a car traveling south on Second Avenue side swiped several parked cars and stopped. Now, Second Avenue is one-way south and 5 lanes wide, with very little traffic at 2:30 in the morning. The driver, likely drunker then we were, got out of the car as we strolled over to inspect the damage.

At this time a passenger got out and was trying to convince the driver to get back in the car and leave. As good citizens we could not let this happen. So I walked up to the driver and suggested he stick around until the cops come. This did not sit well and as a result, he took a round-house punch at my head. Fortunately, he was very drunk and I saw it coming with plenty of time to react. I too was not at the top of my game, but deflected the punch, which appeared to develop in slow motion. Now I became agitated and pushed the driver against a car and was about to do, I don't know what, when the cops arrived.

One of the cops was pulling us apart as the driver was accusing me of assault. I'm thinking: I'm heading to jail. Fortunately Ren convinced the other cop of what actually happened. He walked over to us, told me to go home and stuffed the guilty driver in the back of the cruiser. Another lucky ending. Happy St. Patrick's Day.

20.

LAFAYETTE GRADUATION

THERE WERE MANY UPS and downs through college, but overall, especially in the last two years, I had a charmed life and was reluctant to let it go. Graduation was on June 6, a Friday, Mother's birthday. I thought that appropriate. My gift to her was the diploma. We invited Aunt Dot and Uncle Eddy, my godparents, Phil and Ellen, and of course Leslie, Henry, and Jill. Alayne also came as we were definitely a couple at that point.

Mother arrived Thursday for Baccalaureate and afterward, a group of us went out to dinner. We got back about 9 p.m. and Mother and Alayne went back to the hotel. I went to the Rock Room bar. There were about half a dozen die-hard seniors gathered there, and the beer was running out. Just in time, Ren Drews, who likely had more experience in the Rock Room then I did, came to the rescue with several cases of Rolling Rock, a local favorite. Our last undergraduate party continued long into Friday morning.

Skip woke me at 9 a.m., in our wonderful second floor suite at the fraternity, fully dressed in his uniform. We were to be commissioned in the Army at 11 a.m. followed by graduation at 2 p.m. The plan, the Army always had a plan, was to form up at 10 a.m. and march into Colton Chapel for commissioning. This was a clear case of hurry up and wait, but I had broken enough ROTC rules and hadn't planned on breaking this one. That gave me one hour to get ready.

Normally that would have been plenty of time, but not that morning. I had had my uniform sent out to get cleaned and it was hanging in the closet without any of the Army stuff stuck on (name tag and other assorted doodads). Since I had no idea how these were to be positioned, I made Skip stand still while I copied his uniform. I was hung over and my hands were shaking, so this took quite a while, much to our mutual frustration. After the uniform was ready, I took a shower and began to feel better. Still had time to make it.

As I pulled on my pants, I realized that the inseam of my left leg had become undone from about mid-calf to mid-thigh. This apparently happened at the cleaners and only came to light at this inopportune time. Fortunately, it was on the inside, not the outside of my leg, but I needed several safety pins in the worst sort of way. Most guys had already packed up to leave, so no one was around and no safety pins were found. I finally got to the staging area about 15 minutes late, and we stood around for another 20 minutes before moving into the Colton Chapel for the commissioning. We sat in the first four or five rows, it must have been about 80 guys, with parents, relatives, and friends behind us. Since the Chapel was small, Mother was the only one representing me.

I wanted to make her proud, but was concerned about my pants, and as the event proceeded, I started to feel sick sitting in the hot stuffy chapel. My hat was resting on my lap, upside down, and all I could think about was throwing up in it. Not good, but my only option. As the guest speaker droned on, my situation deteriorated until someone opened a door or window and fresh air entered the chamber. I was saved. Not only did my sick feeling subside, but we walked up to get commissioned in a counterclockwise rotation, which positioned the slit on the inside of my left leg away from the crowd. The Lord was looking out for me that morning.

Outside the Chapel, Mother pinned on my Second Lieutenant bars, making me an Officer and a Gentleman, although both were untested at that moment. I quickly went back to change into civilian clothes for graduation, which was a piece of cake after the Chapel. Our little group had a nice dinner south of Easton in a restaurant along the Delaware River. After dinner Alayne and I were going back to the house to pack and head back home. When I casually mentioned that I still needed to do some packing (I hadn't done any), Ellen volunteered to help.

I didn't want to start packing because that would have acknowledged that college was coming to an end and I didn't like that idea. So it took Alayne, Ellen, Phil, and me some time to pack and fit everything into my little blue VW Beetle. At one point Ellen was cleaning out my top dresser drawer and found an open box of condoms. She turned to me and with a slight smile, asked if I wanted to keep them. I said yes.

College was over, but there were frontiers yet to conquer.

About the Author

RICK MOORE is a Professional Engineer specializing in water pollution control. He is widely published in the field and was President of consulting businesses in the US and India.

Between receiving a Bachelor's degree in Civil Engineering at Lafayette College and a Masters at the University of Maryland, Rick served two years as a Lieutenant in the Army Corps of Engineers, first at Fort Belvior, Virginia and then in Vietnam.

Recently, Rick founded Moore Engineering, a Service Disabled Veteran Owned Small Business, located in Boston MA.